Jethro Tull

HEAVY HORSES

In-depth

Laura Shenton

"I don't want it to just be a formula for Jethro Tull... I might write a song about the sort of thing you shouldn't be singing about, according to the laws of what is successful today. Consequently, I must believe that even though it may not be very successful, I'll write about it anyway."

— Ian Anderson, June 1978

Jethro Tull

HEAVY HORSES

In-depth

Laura Shenton

WYMER
PUBLISHING
Bedford, England

First published in 2022
by Wymer Publishing, Bedford, England
www.wymerpublishing.co.uk Tel: 01234 326691
Wymer Publishing is a trading name of Wymer (UK) Ltd

Print edition (fully illustrated): **ISBN: 978-1-912782-97-0**

Edited by Jerry Bloom.

eBook formatting by Coinlea.

A catalogue record for this book is available from the British Library.

Typeset by Andy Bishop / 1016 Sarpsborg
Cover design by 1016 Sarpsborg.
Cover photo © Pictorial Press / Alamy Stock Photo

Contents

Preface

After *Thick As A Brick* and *Minstrel In The Gallery*, *Heavy Horses* is my third book of the in-depth series featuring a Jethro Tull album. Hardly surprising considering that the story behind each album is one to be told and, most importantly perhaps, Jethro Tull made so many good albums. So of course, I have a bias but as ever, I promise to be objective in providing an exploration into how *Heavy Horses* came to be, how the songs were performed live and what the album means in the context of Jethro Tull's discography overall.

It could be said that compared to *Thick As A Brick* and *Minstrel In The Gallery*, *Heavy Horses* is a less demanding album with less drama behind the scenes regarding the making of it. When Jethro Tull did *Thick As A Brick*, commercially, they were still in a tentative stage of their tenure having gone through several line-up changes and with their fourth album, *Aqualung* (1971) only just having taken them another step up the ladder towards wider commercial success. As a long song across two sides of an LP, *Thick As A Brick* is musically demanding and even amongst the backdrop of progressive rock's popularity at the time, Jethro Tull's 1972 album was a bold move.

Tull's 1975 album, *Minstrel In The Gallery*, was made at a turbulent time for the band. Whilst the line-up remained stable, Ian Anderson wasn't the happiest whilst making the album (as he has been candid about over the years across several interviews). As a result, *Minstrel In The Gallery* is a challenging album based not only on the latter, but in terms of how Jethro Tull were still at an uncertain point in their career from a commercial perspective. 1974's *War Child*, along with the hit single from it, 'Bungle In The Jungle', had been seen as something of a comeback from the badly panned *A Passion Play* (1973). Thus when it came to *Minstrel In The Gallery*, things could have gone either way for the band. In particular, some of the material on that album still harks back to their long-song days with the almost sixteen minute 'Baker Street Muse' but equally, there are shorter songs too — many of which make excellent use of Martin Barre's straight-up rock style electric guitar.

So of course, by 1978, Jethro Tull were in a very different place as a band. They had gone on quite the journey to establish themselves commercially. There had certainly been an abundance of ups and downs. Essentially, commercially they'd done the groundwork and musically their trademark sound had been solidified in the public consciousness. Regardless of thematic changes in each of their albums across the seventies, by 1978, people probably had a strong idea of what to expect.

Due to this, there is less drama to report with regards to the making of *Heavy Horses* and indeed the album's success. Nevertheless there is relevance in exploring it all here because from an archiving perspective and a music appreciation perspective, it matters. *Heavy Horses* was still a brave album for Jethro Tull to do in view of the unusual theme, use of folk music and the fact that by the late seventies, there was a lot of interesting variety emerging in terms of which genres of music were commercially in demand.

Anyhow, on the archiving front, as with my previous books, you will see lots of quotes from a range of sources. What was said about *Heavy Horses* at the time of its production, release and performance (both by Jethro Tull and others) is important; I feel it is an effective way to provide an authentic perspective. As with the other books, this isn't an exercise in putting my own opinion across. In such regard, there will still be no "this song is in B minor so it probably means XYZ." A good few years ago now though, I did manage to get hold of the sheet music book — published by Almo in 1978 under license from Chrysalis — for *Heavy Horses* and due to that, I have endeavoured to list some facts about that in the index of this book. The changes of time signature in most Jethro Tull songs are a source of fascination and it would be a missed opportunity not to share them with you here (the sheet music book is sadly very hard to get hold of having been out of print for so long — although just scored for piano and vocals, it really is such an eye-opener). The time signatures show that Jethro Tull were ever the innovators when it came to creativity.

In 1978, Ian Anderson was doing most of the public speaking on behalf of Jethro Tull and the proportion of band member quotes in this book is reflective of that. As I have mentioned before and in the interest of continued transparency, I have no affiliation with anyone from Jethro Tull and/or with any of their associates.

Chapter One

Why Heavy Horses?

By 1978, Jethro Tull had been going for ten years. The band had built a solid reputation on the likes of albums such as *Aqualung* (1971) and *Thick As A Brick* (1972). Although the mid-seventies had been a bit hit and miss for them, commercially, they had remained strong as a live act, had a keen following of fans and were still succeeding to put out a new album every year.

Released in April 1978, *Heavy Horses* was Jethro Tull's eleventh studio album. It demonstrated strongly that creatively, the band were still very much at the top of their game. An endearing mix of themes and musical ideas both from the past and the present, *Heavy Horses* is an eclectic album that draws on a range of influences: folk, rock, and hard rock in particular.

It was Jethro Tull's 1977 album, *Songs From The Wood* that had really put the band's use of folk influences on the map with tracks such as 'Fire At Midnight', 'Jack-In-The-Green', 'The Whistler' and the title track. With *Heavy Horses*, Jethro Tull continued to run with the folk theme, as is evident on 'Moths' and 'Acres Wild'. 'Weathercock' is a fine example of the melding of folk and hard rock that takes place on *Heavy Horses*.

By many, *Heavy Horses* is considered to be part of a trio of albums that are musically in the same vein: *Songs From The Wood*, *Heavy Horses* and *Stormwatch* (1979). (That said, some consider that *Stormwatch* made something of a move away from the rural theme and thus see *Songs From The Wood* and *Heavy Horses* as a pair).

Either way, the late seventies were an iconic period for Jethro Tull and *Heavy Horses* sits there comfortably as a strong album for 1978. Anderson told *Prog* in March 2018; "It was fairly hot on the heels of the *Songs From The Wood* album. In my mind, *Heavy Horses* is a logical successor — not quite part two, but it follows on with that slightly more rural context of its predecessor for a lot of the songs."

As with all of Jethro Tull's seventies albums, *Heavy Horses* is abundant in Ian Anderson's distinctive vocals and use of flute. With that, there is plenty of beautiful acoustic guitar teamed thoughtfully with electric guitar — all driven by energetic percussion.

Ian Anderson's tales of living in the countryside are an innovative interpretation of the social and cultural aspects of rural life — both from a present and past perspective. Some might say that the subject matter on *Heavy Horses* is darker than that on *Songs From The Wood*. The brutal aspect of nature is certainly put in the spotlight. There is also a sense of romantic nostalgia for an era gone by.

In the newspaper advert for *Heavy Horses*, Chrysalis described it as follows: "Soon the heavy horses will be coming home... *Heavy Horses* is the new album from Jethro Tull. Just one album ago, the world discovered a new and different Ian Anderson. Still exhibiting his wonderfully wicked sense of humour, *Songs From The Wood* also lovingly took a musical tour of the English countryside. *Heavy Horses*, dedicated to the Shires, Percherons and Suffolks that were once the backbone of rural England, travels through the same pastoral country of today exploring even newer directions. Musically it's one of Tull's best albums, Ian Anderson's lyrics being as sharp and perceptive as ever. Included on the album you'll find the single 'Moths' which has 'Life Is A Long Song' on the B-side, and if you're lucky, you'll be able to see Jethro Tull on their forthcoming sold out UK tour. In the meantime, take a listen to the album. *Heavy Horses* is one worth coming home to."

A week after its release, *Heavy Horses* peaked at number twenty in the UK chart. By 1978, there was an exciting range of music dominating the radio airwaves. Punk, new wave and disco were in their element. From a commercial perspective, it could be considered that *Heavy Horses* was a tremendous risk; musically, there was nothing else like it at the time. Maybe that is something that went very much in Jethro Tull's favour though, especially in terms of how they were already liked by many specifically due to their unique signature sound. Still though, when 'Moths' was released as a single, it failed to chart. Not only that, but some of the reviews were a little derogatory.

'Moths' was reviewed in *Record Mirror* in April 1978; "Whitesmock haychewing-turningthesodcalfstroking-rockaboo (sic). A single from the soil, for dancing around the campfire, Anderson intones a story of awakening summer (c'mon get out of bed) and moths gathering around the flame. Reminds you of sunrises and sunsets in deepest Berkshire, the roll of the hills and the birds black against the sunlit sky. Hopping acoustic guitar playing that had left me flat on my back and then the old flute trademark. B-side is the evergreen 'Life Is A Long Song' timely reissue of the hit single a few years back. Pass the flagon of cider."

Regarding his policy on singles by that point, Anderson told *Beat Instrumental* in May 1978; "I regard them as trailers for the album, not as anything else. I don't have the ability, and certainly not the inclination, to write instant two and a half minute songs. What I would really like is a single in the top twenty — at about number nineteen. A single at number three would horrify me. God knows we've already got a younger audience which is posing difficulties of its own. The older people aren't going to gigs anymore, and they've been replaced by these very young rock 'n' roll audiences — difficult to play to as well. A lot of the old songs leave them cold as it's before their time."

Sensibly perhaps, the 'Moths' single wasn't given a release in the US. Maybe it could have done okay though. After all, *Heavy Horses* got to number nineteen in the US. Notably, Jethro Tull's engagement with American audiences would be particularly strong throughout the whole of 1978, as their touring schedule and gig reviews demonstrate.

Anderson told *Prog* in March 2018; "You have to remember, this was at the time punk's final embers were burning out and you had bands like The Police and The Stranglers, who were, collectively speaking, a bunch of old hippies. The brave new world of punk rock had perhaps become commercialised at that point. But bands like those two used punk as a means to get their foot in the door, just as I did with the blues in 1968. So from our perspective then, it wasn't that we were vindicated that this new, intrusive music form had somehow ousted us from the public eye and approval, it was just a parallel event. I don't really recall being moved as a music maker by any of those changes in music that were going on. I knew what it was about and I rather liked some of it, but it was entirely separate to what I was writing. I didn't want to try to catch up or be influenced by it. We were still making Jethro Tull albums at that point."

Ian Anderson certainly wasn't disparaging of what was commercially popular at the time. He was quoted on his opinion of Ian Dury in *Record Mirror* in May 1978; "He's been very clever in getting involved in the Stiff thing. I heard a song called 'My Old Man'. The lyrics were very good and you could identify with them. He's able to put across a very clear thought."

Anderson told *Sounds* in June 1977; "I heard the Sex Pistols song on the radio the other day and what little I could make out of the lyrics, at least I heard some aggressive, nasty-sounding English voices and I thought 'That's refreshing', at least they're not listening to that mind-boggling top forty pseudo-American Epsom that you hear all the time on British radio. I'll give the Sex Pistols a listen, if they're singing in their own natural street voices. Just for that alone I would listen to them."

Besides, was punk really *that different* to what had gone before? Anderson told *Creem* in June 1978; "It's a shame that the punk rock thing is so laden with the fact that it's very derivative musically of things that you and I are familiar with — the rock, the riffs, the beat. We've all heard and experienced it probably twice already. Punk rock is just another time for the same old tried and tested elementary rock riff, same old electric guitar, same old drum kit set up the same old way. And it's so class-ridden, "the music of the working class". The great thing when I came in was that it was classless. It was great back then. People did cross the borders of style and class. But the punk thing is a working-class thing and so you only get someone hyphen something following punk out of a terrible mixed-up rebellious thing."

In 1978, to make an album about horses and life in the English countryside was a commercial risk. There was still room for progressive rock though; it was in the same year that Yes and Genesis were both at the top of their game with *Tomato* and *...And Then There Were Three...* respectively. Would Jethro Tull have faired as well had they not worked so hard to achieve international stardom earlier on in the decade? Well, maybe not. Thankfully though, the audience was there to be had and as a result, *Heavy Horses* was successful in 1978 and as a snapshot into Jethro Tull's overall tenure, it stands up well today. In fact, many fans consider it to be one of Tull's best.

Anderson told BBC Radio in March 1979; "The sort of issues that I could be publicly angry about don't readily translate into pop music. I mean it would be silly of me to start putting forward political (or anything like political) views that I might hold, and to be trying seriously to deal with other issues. It's the wrong time, now. If I want to do that I ought to be either a politician or a sleeping politician and write books about it, but not in terms of these songs. I think I'm dealing more with fantasy, and interpretations of things that otherwise might be taken for granted. I really don't want to use rock music as a social or political platform, doing a sort of latter-day Bob Dylan. It would amuse me to do that, but I don't think it would go down well with anybody and quite rightly so. It would upset me if I heard somebody else using their fame, as it were, I mean no one really liked it when John Lennon started getting into that rather aggressive, pseudo-political approach. Everybody got turned off, didn't they? And quite rightly."

So who were Jethro Tull's audience by 1978? Anderson admitted to *Creem* in the June of that year; "I've really no idea who they are and I've really no idea what they like about us. I posed this question on the last tour in America, particularly at the end of last year's tour, because the audience was so overwhelmingly young again. There was this incredible element of fifteen and sixteen-year-old kids there, who would have been seven or eight when we started and I don't know why they're there because why aren't they supporting the trendy up-and-comings? Why aren't they supporting their own heroes instead of latching on to the heroes of the generation before them? I don't know the answer."

"I find it distinctively worrying. I'm very gratified that they're there and people say I should be really pleased because this is your audience for the next five or ten years — you've actually broken that age barrier, they're yours. But I still find it worrying. I find it worrying because why weren't the Sex Pistols doing it already? Why aren't all the other groups who've had a go and haven't made it? In America particularly, and on the world stage, there still seems to be this handful of groups and most of them are British. It's your problem as a sociologist and it's my problem only in that I feel some responsibility for the fact that they're there, perhaps getting beaten up or mugged on their way home. That's the only way it worries me, because I can't really probe into the whys and wherefores of who they are and the reasons they like Jethro Tull. I don't know."

He told *Circus* in November 1978; "Suddenly we've lost the older age group to their domesticity, their mortgages, their family cars, and half a swimming pool average. But it's left a free space for a much younger audience to come in and surprisingly they do. I've queried as to why they come to see Jethro Tull, why they don't want to find their own younger groups to follow. And the only explanation that makes any sense is that, like the Stones or The Who, Jethro Tull has a certain reputation, a mystique that's transcended the generation gap."

And *National Rock Star* in February 1977; "I am flattered to find a changing audience. I see people drifting away at the upper end of the age spectrum because they have other priorities in life, like mortgage repayments and children on the way, etc. It's probably better to take the wife to the pictures one night a week than buy that new rock album. On the other hand, at the other end of the age scale, we get an influx of people around the fifteen and sixteen mark, which mostly happens in America."

A key thing that *Heavy Horses* had going for it when it was realised in 1978 is originality; whilst many bands who were at their peak in the early seventies were simply going through the motions by the late seventies, Ian Anderson was writing lyrics and coming up with ideas that still brought something original to the table. (Emerson, Lake and Palmer's *Love Beach* springs to mind here — released in late 1978, it got to number forty-eight in the UK and whilst that's not bad going and chart positions aren't everything, their first four albums all hit within the top five. By 1978 though, ELP were not working happily together).

Even though prog rock's peak in popularity had somewhat passed by 1978, importantly for Jethro Tull, they had a good promotional team behind them. In March 1978, *Billboard* reported that "Chrysalis is to release five albums in April including LPs from Jethro Tull, Mary O'Hara, Steve Hackett, Frankie Miller and Auracle" to which it was stated "There will also be an extensive marketing and merchandising campaign centred around the new Tull release, titled *Heavy Horses*."

In the same month, *Billboard* reported on the steps being taken to support *Heavy Horses*: "For the new Jethro Tull album, the label is making twenty-three by thirty-five inch full catalogue posters, special posters of the new album as well as canvas type posters. The latter will be a limited edition which will go to radio and retailers. Also for Tull will be a special gold paperweight in horseshoe form to tie in with its new album, *Heavy Horses*."

Amongst many things, by 1978, it was plausibly to Jethro Tull's commercial advantage that they had remained, overall, prolific and popular in the mid-seventies. In particular, they had a hit with the single 'Ring Out, Solstice Bells' in December 1976. It got to number twenty-eight. It was released prior to the album it features on, *Songs From The Wood* and had seen the band perform on *Top Of The Pops*. Anderson had told *Sounds* in January 1976; "At the back of the old fiendish brain there lurks something in me that wants to go on *Top Of The Pops*. I don't know why. I think I'll do it again. Have a hit single."

Anderson told BBC Radio in March 1979; "I wanted to write a Christmas song, but, you know, I was damned if I was going to write a Christmas song about Christianity. I wanted to write a song about what Christmas really is all about, which is something way before that, before the Christians adopted the date — try to put something of the joy of the original Christmas festivity into a song which is seemingly innocuous. But really the thought behind that is directed very much against the idea of the Christian Christmas festival."

Of course, the success of 'Ring Out, Solstice Bells' did wonders for the promotion of *Songs From The Wood* and importantly, it was a generally well-received album (despite some of the less than complementary reviews). It got to number thirteen in the UK and to number eight in the US — an excellent platform on which Jethro Tull could build by the time it came to making and promoting *Heavy Horses*.

It was considered in *Circus* in April 1977; "Jethro Tull's *Songs From The Wood* is a fresh breath of medieval air, as modern as it is ancient and traditional. 'I want to produce an album which is different from anything we've done before,' Ian Anderson mused over his breakfast some time ago at New York's Regency Hotel. 'It'll be less blues and more of some particularly British hybrid form — more modal, more Celtic. I find the music I'm writing now embodies something of the very earliest musical tradition, an almost religious music of celebration. I want to try to evoke something a little more spiritual and emotional.' *Songs From The Wood*, Jethro Tull's latest Chrysalis release, is Anderson's bid to fulfil that stated aim. Always a Heavy Elizabethan band drawing more from the old folk tradition than rhythm and blues, Jethro Tull have given the new LP an even more pronounced medieval flavouring than gaieties of the past."

"With Anderson's hedonistic lyrics, the set has the thematic aura of a collection of organic, sixteenth century pastorals. Jethro Tull's idiosyncratic and rarely imitated sound springs from the personality of Ian Anderson, whose whole adult life has been characterised by a streak of non-conformity... *Songs From The Wood* is probably like no other album that will be released in 1977. The title tune opens as an a cappella madrigal and then proceeds with choppy pageantry. 'Jack-In-The-Green' is the protest of a leprechaun figure troubled by the encroachment of modern civilisation (reminds me of 'Morris In Chains' from Robert Coover's magical book, *Pricksongs & Descants*). 'Cup Of Wonder' is a mild, melodic feasting air suitable for digesting a little Sherwood Forest venison."

"The last two numbers on side one are the oddest of the LP. 'Hunting Girl' involves strange sexual tastes (Anderson uses a whip as a prop on this one), while 'Ring Out, Solstice Bells' is a celebration of Christmas cheer. Side two opens with 'Velvet Green', an idyllic, harpsichord-laced trysting piece. It's adorned with mist, lowing cows, the scent of wild roses, and 'your legs in the air, walking on velvet green' in a Scotch pine grove. 'The Whistler' is a carpe diem seduction ('I have a fife and I've come to play') reminding us that Britain's first rocker was Andrew Marvell (1621-78). 'Pibroch (Cap In Hand)' is a longish, heavy lament, by definition a martial bagpipe air, but unfortunately Ian passes up the opportunity to employ the regal sounding windbags. The capper on the album is 'Fire At

Midnight', a comfortable, fulfilled song about dying embers and going upstairs and folding your clothes — a lulling fade-out on Ian Anderson's *Midsummer Night's Dream.*"

Songs From The Wood was reviewed in *Sounds* in February 1977; "If you play this album at 45rpm it sounds just like Steeleye Span. If you then change the speed control and spin it again it sounds just as much like Cat Stevens backed by Fairport Convention at the execution of Babbacombe Lee. Yes, friends, Jethro Tull have revamped their old medieval image. In fact, if you believe the press kit that accompanies *Songs From The Wood*, this latest album marks Jethro Tull's 'return to the earth, and for that matter, their roots'. In fact, far from being a return to the roots, *Songs From The Wood* is in fact just one more in the line of "concept albums" that started, somewhat hesitantly, with *Aqualung*. In many respects it's as good as all the others."

"You come to expect a certain level of competence and expertise from Tull, even when they're substandard. There's less of Martin Barre's ferocious electric guitar on this album and many more acoustic instruments than usual, but the production and the playing is well over par. The unaccompanied voices and then the sweeping guitar on the title track are extremely attractive, while 'Ring Out, Solstice Bells' is every bit as strong as the best from Tull's early years. The rest offer the customary bait of strange tempo changes, rich tones and Anderson's trademark, his double-track and slightly vibrated vocal mix."

"But as a concept album in the great tradition of concept albums it has absolutely nothing to say. Admittedly Ian Anderson has always been rock's Herman Hesse, a schoolboy intellectual with a particularly florid and attractive style. Yet *Aqualung* did burst a blood vessel or two over urban insecurity, and *Thick As A Brick* upstaged the Sex Pistols by about five years. One should not refuse Anderson some of the relevance and achievement he seems to think has been denied him. *Songs From The Wood* then uses as its framework that often highly nebulous music that passes for "period" when considering the dark ages before widespread literacy. But with a distinctly medieval taste to it."

"If track titles like 'Cup Of Wonder', 'Jack-In-The-Green', 'The Whistler', 'Velvet Green', 'Pibroch (Cap In Hand)' and the Christmas single 'Ring Out, Solstice Bells' don't evoke the same romantic vision of a by-gone age as Jay Lee's cover paintograph, then spin the record and listen to the words and the music. Literary archetypes from pre-theatrical drama and local legend walk down the old straight track as Ian Anderson follows the keylines of Old English balladry with instruments and tunes to suit. But unfortunately the whole affair sounds like the background music to TV's *Robin Hood*, the score of a movie like *Tom Jones* or perhaps the lowlife themes from *Barry Lyndon*."

"Shot in Technicolor through gauze they may be, but they mean little or nothing alone. Steeleye Span play the same game but they succeed because they have strong control over the authenticity of their material. And, at heart, Maddy P. and the boys are well aware that in its original form their music was never meant to be more than a form of community-based entertainment. But on this album Ian Anderson sounds even more soulful and intense than usual. Sometimes he sounds as cloying as Cat Stevens. But he seems to have nothing to say to justify the emotional weight he's throwing about. After the heavy leather bias of the last album *Too Old To Rock 'n' Roll: Too Young To Die* it is hard to see *Songs From The Wood* as more than just a well-prepared exercise in style. If Tommy Garrett and his Fifty Guitars can play Hawaiian and James Last can play the Beatles then Jethro Tull can turn to

Traditional Folk. Maybe the next one will be Latin American in flavour."

Songs From The Wood was reviewed in *Record Mirror* in February 1977; "Welcome to CAMRA, the Campaign for Rustic Anthems, brought to your ears courtesy of ye olde Ian Anderson Band, otherwise known as Jethro Tull. CAMRA albums come out, on average, once a year, and are all too often compared to the classic *Aqualung* of several summers ago. This latest brew, as the label suggests, features a selection of songs with strong rural flavours. Jolly mandolins, the flute — the trademark of all CAMRA products — and Squire Anderson's vocals potter their way through a selection of rhymes and ditties. Bonus ingredients are their last special single brew 'Ring Out, Solstice Bells' and their next 'The Whistler'. When you hold this brew up to the light, you should be able to see through it with little trouble. It has a mellow taste as of autumn leaves tinged with rabbit stew. Over-indulgence can lead to a headache and other symptoms known collectively as a hangover (from the sixties?) Three pints of ordinary, please."

It was reviewed in *Melody Maker* in January 1977; "Here we go again. Loath as I am to raise the subject, and loath as Ian Anderson is to accept it, it is a simple fact of life that a little masterpiece called *Aqualung* was easily the most successful and forceful work recorded by Jethro Tull. It's been said before — and it will be again — that until Tull reach a height that is comparable to the scintillating pitch you-know-what touched, then everything they do will live in its shadow. *Songs From The Wood* could have been swallowed by this ominous shadow, were it not for the fact that although it comes nowhere near striking the same high, it does manage to sow seeds on which Tull can build and, in perhaps a couple of albums' time, reach this elusive climax again."

"Why the optimism? Well, although this is only a fairly good, occasionally very good and-once-brilliant album, it can be justifiably argued that *Songs From The Wood* is the first of a new-age Tull recording. It is definitely unlike anything they have recorded before. Perhaps Ian Anderson has decided to put his money where his often over-sized mouth is, and really attempt to vary the formula. The three albums he has made since his "comeback", *War Child, Minstrel In The Gallery* and *Too Old To Rock 'n' Roll: Too Young To Die*, are practically all negligible contributions to the Tull repertoire, although *Minstrel In The Gallery* holds its head above water in the long term by providing a couple of classics in the shape of 'Black Satin Dancer', 'One White Duck' and 'Mother England Reverie', as well as being vaguely reminiscent of the Tull of the *Aqualung* period we all wanted to hear."

"*Songs From The Wood* is more durable than its three predecessors, probably because Anderson and his band start fiddling adventurously with the formula, kicking it around and coming up with more experimental arrangements. As well as that, Anderson's vocal blends in much more with the arrangement than it has done. It really sounds as if it is part of the songs. But before going any further, I'll refer to the discrepancies which make it only a fairly good album. First, there's the hideous concept, because these really are songs from the wood, and their substance never has much bite or attack. And anyway, Ian Anderson as Robin Hood, or even as the country squire on the sleeve, doesn't appeal to me. That's really bland. Really boring."

"Coming as this does, then, from the wood, it's relevant that much of the instrumental music on the album is very folk-orientated, with lutes, whistles and, of course, flutes. Tull's attempts, however, at scoring a folk symphony on 'Velvet Green' or just playing the dumb folkie on 'Jack-In-The-

Green', where he sings incredibly in the style of Cat Stevens, and 'The Whistler', getting a good old-fashioned jig together, are shallow. That side of the material is just plain weak. The optimism on *Songs From The Wood* stems from four tracks: 'Cup Of Wonder', 'Hunting Girl', 'Fire At Midnight' and 'Pibroch (Cap In Hand)'. 'Pibroch' is easily the album's superlative cut, a gutsy Tull rocker with a haunting build-up. It opens with a grinding riff from Barre on the guitar and Evans on synthesiser, drops to a taunting Anderson vocal and creeps back in at various times, with the impact sharpened even more by Anderson's flute line. One of the sadder aspects of this album, in fact, is that Martin Barre is never set loose, which seems to me to be a sad waste of talent, although one of the better aspects of the tracks — and 'Pibroch' in particular — is the contribution of the band to the arrangements, especially keyboardists Evans and Palmer. 'Cup Of Wonder' and 'Hunting Girl', placed side by side on the album, are snappy, melodic Anderson compositions, and judging by the positive feel on the two, were recorded when the band were in a very enthusiastic mood. The acoustic guitar/flute riff on 'Cup Of Wonder' is neat, and 'Hunting Girl' is beautifully punctuated throughout by Barre's jabbing phrases and Glascock's busy bass."

"On almost every album, Anderson comes up with a lovely mellow tune. 'Fire At Midnight' is the one on this album. As a sticker on the sleeve will probably announce: 'Includes the hit single, 'Ring Out, Solstice Bells'', to which I'm totally indifferent. *Songs From The Wood* won't restore Tull's flagging prestige in Britain. Nor will it be seen as a real downer. Its place lies somewhere in-between those two poles — an offering from a band that displays new potential without fully realising it. File under "reasonably popular"."

In April 1978, an advert placed by Chrysalis in *Billboard*

stated; "Following the great success of *Songs From The Wood*, Ian Anderson has produced another musical tour of the English countryside. Bigger and better, *Heavy Horses* travels through the same pastoral country, exploring new musical directions. The album contains all the musical nuances that have endeared Jethro Tull to millions of buyers and audiences over the years."

For the making of *Heavy Horses*, the personnel dynamics within Jethro Tull were such that bandleader Ian Anderson and guitarist Martin Barre were the main initiators of the group's overall sound. With them though, was a strong line-up. David Palmer (now known as Dee Palmer but referred to in this book as how he was credited at the time) was on keyboards, portative pipe organ and orchestral arrangements having contributed some amazing arrangements since *This Was* in 1968. Still with the band since April 1970 and May 1971 respectively, were John Evan on piano and organ and Barriemore Barlow on drums. Having joined the band and having fitted in well since 1976 was John Glascock on bass guitar.

Overall, *Heavy Horses* is a charming album and one that shows Jethro Tull at a creative and commercial peak.

Jethro Tull Stands Its Creative Ground

By GREG BEEBE
Sentinel Staff Writer

Quick. Name a rock band still around after 10 years of existence. Rock music is not noted for the durability of its exponents, and only a handful of bands can attest to being successful in both the '60s and '70s. At the rate Jethro Tull is going, this avant-garde rock group could extend its popularity into the '80s.

Record Review

Not that Jethro Tull hasn't gone through the turmoil, personality conflicts and personnel changes so common to the trade. But, with the innovative leadership of flutist Ian Anderson, the band has been able to stand its creative ground while the New Wave washes away other supposedly "estab-

lished" bands.

Jethro Tull has released 14 albums in 10 years, five of which went platinum, 11 of which went gold. "Heavy Horses" is Tull's latest release.

JETHRO TULL: "Heavy Horses," Chrysalis Records — "Heavy Horses" was certified as a gold album even before it was released. That is because the record is sure to sell at least 100,000 copies as soon as it hits the racks. Jethro Tull has a large and chauvinistic following obsessed with collecting all the band's recorded works.

The six-man ensemble is led by Anderson, whose vocals, acoustic guitar and spine-tingling flute are the backbone of the band.

Tull's sound is exquisitely executed with great attention paid to instrumentation and lyrical themes. Jethro Tull fuses tell a story, and each album is a

small volume of stories.

The title track of "Heavy Horses" is a sensitive appeal to shire horses, which like seemingly everything else are threatened these days.

The mood changes in the upbeat rock-blues number "The Mouse Police Never Sleeps," and the soft ballad, "Moths." Anderson pretty much sums up the music of Jethro Tull when he says, "I don't want to sing songs that other people are singing; that's for certain. I don't want to make rock 'n' roll music that somebody else has already done. I want to do something different.

GLIDER: "Glider," United Artists Records — With record albums becoming more and more expensive, buyers are considerably less willing to 'take a chance" on a certain effort when there are plenty of proven artists on the shelves.

Glider, a relatively new band from the east coast, is good enough to warrant a listen. Although not particularly new or different, the music of Ted Myers (guitar, vocals), Gene Barkin (guitar) Jeff Eyrich (bass) and Ed Tuduri (drums) has a light and airy rock sound with emphasis on two and three-part vocal harmonies.

Songs like "Midnight Rider" combine forceful guitars with feathery vocals, mixing elements of folk, blues, jazz and mostly rock.

If you don't mind having a noname on your turntable, Glider is worth a chance and maybe even a pleasant surprise.

Greenpeace Film

Representatives from Greenpeace, the group which has been fighting to stop the slaughter of whales by

Japanese and Russian fishermen, will be at Cabrillo College to show a film 'Voyages to Save the Whales," Saturday, May 6, 7:30 p.m. in forum 450.

Tull's Feast Is Fit For A King

BY CLIFF RADEL
Enquirer Pop Music Critic

The king and queen sat with their court in the castle's great hall. A fire blazed on the hearth. Empty plates covered the royal table. The feast was over.

"Bring on the entertainment," commanded the king.

A traveling troupe of musicians trooped onto the stage.

The leader strummed guitar, played flute and sang. Another played lute, another bass lute. Yet another shook tambourines and pounded drums covered with rawhide heads. Two other musicians tended primitive clavichords.

The flutist twirled his instrument and jabbed it at his regal audience.

POOF!

The castle, the great hall, the hearth, the court, the queen and her king vanished.

In their place, Wednesday night, stood Riverfront Coliseum and 13,300 spectators. The leader retained his instruments. The lutists traded theirs for electric lead and bass guitars. The tambourine shaker and pounder of rawhide drum heads switched to a set of late-20th century drums, cymbals and glockenspiel. The clavichords aged, electri-

fied and multiplied to become synthesizers, harpsichords, clavinets, electric pianos, organs and one portative pipe organ. Parts of the group's songs remained unchanged. In the turmoil, the troupe acquired a name — Jethro Tull.

Medieval magic was not behind this rush through the ages Jethro Tull's music was. The material performed by the band's leader, Ian Anderson, and his fellow Tullians created the impression they had just gotten off a flight from the Middle Ages.

"AQUALUNG," the first of Jethro Tull's two encores, which capped the sextet's 82-minute performance, offered a fine example of rock from the Middle Ages as imagined through the ears of 20th century Englishmen.

The song began with six ominous notes. This figure, belted out by keyboardists John Evan and David Palmer, guitarist Martin Barre, bass guitarist Anthony Williams and drummer Barriemore Barlow, heralded Anderson's vocal. At this point rock prevailed.

Anderson introduced his character, "Aqualung." This gent looked a mess with "snot running down his nose" and "greasy fingers smearing shabby clothes." Such lyrical con-

tent could only be handled by rock Opera, Broadway musicals and never touch it.

By setting heretofore unteachable subjects to music, Anderson and Tull further substantiate rock claims that, like literature of the 1920s, this energetic idiom knows no thematic bounds.

For the refrain, Anderson turns to the Middle Ages. His voice quivered with turns, trills and grace notes in the time-honored tradition of medieval troubadours. His accom-

Chapter Two

The Making Of Heavy Horses

Regarding the songs on *Heavy Horses*, Anderson told BBC Radio in March 1979; "Well, once again they've been written everywhere. Some of them have been written in hotels on tours during the last twelve months. I usually try to write at least one song on the train, out from Marylebone station to the other end, and I did that again, so there's another train song. One or two I have actually written at home, surrounded by animals and goodness knows what else. The thing is, it's always easier to write songs about your own surroundings and your own real feelings not when you're in the middle of them but when you're sitting in the Holiday Inn or wherever it might be, because then you have a far more objective look at your own life, or the lives of other people for that matter too. The artificiality of the Holiday Inn room existence is an incredible bonus — I mean, just think what works of pure wonder Beethoven would have turned in had he been ensconced in the Holiday Inn, Miami, for the last ten years of his life — half a dozen more symphonies."

As was typical of Ian Anderson's songwriting habits, some of the songs on *Heavy Horses* were written whilst he was commuting. In the case of this album, it was often done whilst he was on the train in and around London. He told *Record Mirror* in May 1978; "I used to do a lot of travelling on trains and I find them good to write songs on. You can lock yourself away in a first-class compartment and you don't feel silly about writing things down on pieces of paper. The rhythm of the train is quite stimulating as well."

And *Prog* in March 2018; "I do remember writing on the train, yes. In most cases the songs for *Heavy Horses* were written before we went into the studio, but sometimes they were written the night before, which is the way I often tend to work: writing things based on yesterday's rehearsal. It will make me rethink something and come up with a new idea or even a new song. I wake up very early in the morning and I work quickly — that's my time to get things done."

Even amongst the abundance of songs with a rural theme on *Heavy Horses*, 'Journeyman' is certainly reflective of someone doing a commute. The song showcases the talent in the band in how it begins with a funky bass line from John Glascock and then flows into something that is beautifully textured with what the other musicians add to it.

Anderson told BBC Radio in March 1979; "The only song that actually alludes to anything British is a song called 'Journeyman', which is the train song I told you about. Just one of those late night, the last train back from Marylebone, which usually contains your businessmen who've usually been out on an expenses dinner, or who have told the wife it was a business dinner, and they're lurching home rather drunk and rather late on the last train, and they've just realised they've got to get all these accounts sorted out by tomorrow. Eleven o'clock at night and their briefcases are open and they're still frantically trying to get things sorted out that they've got to hand in the next day when they go back. And I only mention Gerrards Cross in it once because that always amuses me. It's just hilarious. I'm already on the train, and at Gerrards Cross the carriage fills with these people. And you're always sitting in the seat that one of them customarily occupies, and it's his seat, and you get daggers because the seat he has every day has been taken."

By July 1977, Jethro Tull had recently completed a five month tour of the US and Europe. Having successfully promoted *Songs From The Wood* with this tour, they went back home to get to work on the next album. Anderson's home at the time was in the countryside and elements of that way of living were strongly at the front of his mind. As he was writing the songs for what would become *Heavy Horses*, themes of the rural — farming, animals, nature, agriculture — were all part of his day-to-day life and as such, a strong source of inspiration.

Anderson had moved to the countryside in 1976 having purchased a working farm in rural Buckinghamshire. This had an influence on *Songs From The Wood*. Anderson recalled, "I wrote *Songs From The Wood* based on elements of folklore and fantasy tales and traditions of the British rural environment. You might describe *Songs From The Wood* as a contemporary folk-rock album, in the sense that it's a rock album but it has some sort of folky feel, and it doesn't owe really anything at all to blues or jazz or any black American music."

Of course, an interest in folk music didn't spring up out of the blue. Anderson had already embraced the genre wholeheartedly when producing Steeleye Span's 1974 album, *Now We Are Six*.

In response to being questioned about traditional English folk music, Anderson told *Creem* in July 1977; "I don't listen to anything. I hate that approach, personally speaking. The academic delving and the subtle sharpness of traditional English music is a relatively sterile intellectual exercise. I believe first and foremost in a folk memory. I'm of particularly mixed origin; my mother is English, my father is Scottish. And yet my Scottish family is Anderson, which probably only dates from the tenth to the twelfth century when the Vikings came over to the coast of Scotland and settled — stole the women and whatever else. There were some very attractive birds in that part and they spawned the likes of me. So you have the peculiar sort of mixture of origins in me."

"But I do believe in a folk memory or something which is at once Anglo-Saxon and Celtic mixed together from way back a long, long time ago and I believe that we retain something of, certainly not the academic wherewithal to put that type of music together, but something of the emotional response to that music. There's no point in me any longer pretending to sing the American blues, the black man's music, because that's not what I feel. I have great admiration for it; it's certainly the music of the past fifty years that's given the most in terms of influence to popular music today. But I think that there is a tremendously neglected area of music that stems basically from the pre-history of Europe. You know, I'm talking about the post-Neolithic era where there was civilisation indigenous to quite isolated parts of Britain and some of France."

"There is a particularly religious significance attached to all of this; the worship of the old god, the god of nature. Not the devil, not the fallen angel Lucifer, but the god of nature as most religions tend to talk about him. The god of sunlight, the god of the good harvest, the god of wrath, love, lust — but not in an evil, black magic way. It's just literally the animal truth of what we all are and this is all mixed up as well in the origins of our music. I think it is also mixed up in the origins of the black man's music although he's several thousand miles away and given to a rhythmic approach rather than the melodic one, which is where all this kind of music comes from. Again, Scottish people, or the Celtic thing which was later translated into bagpipe music, which really only comes from 1300 or 1400 onwards and only really took on any significance as a scholarly approach to music in 1600 within the clans. It obviously bears tremendous comparison to that peculiarly sort of religious music of the English culture."

Anderson said on BBC Radio in March 1979; "In *Songs From The Wood* we did go back to the roots of what our music was about, at the same time avoiding what had become the clichés of blues as spawned by the Americans. It's a peculiarly British sounding album, but is in no way a traditional, academic interpretation of old folk song; I mean it's not a Steeleye Span number at all. It's something else — it's still my songs... You know, it's a nice album, it's a very nice album; I really like the album... A couple of years ago I settled down, bought a house, got married, and had a baby. Not necessarily in that order, but almost."

"It's obviously indicative of my mental state at the time, and the other guys too, because we'd all settled down in Britain, accepted the fact that we were going to pay enormous percentages of our income in tax, came to realise that that has to be, that we did not want to become tax exiles and live in Liechtenstein or the Bahamas or whatever other place had been suggested to us. So, there comes about a general acceptance and an enjoyment of our environment; I don't mean just in the sense of living in the country, but in the sense of Britain as a whole. We have in *Songs From The Wood* a situation in which I'm trying on the one hand not to be socially critical, on the other hand trying to keep some of the musical roots of which the group is known for. I'm really trying to express some sort of joy, in all the songs... It's all done in a warm way, a tongue-in-cheek way: there's nothing bitter, there's no sort of social critique involved there at all."

Heavy Horses was Jethro Tull's first album to be recorded at Maison Rouge. Anderson had built the studio in 1977. Opening it in the June of that year, it was perfect timing for the band to start working there. He told *Prog* in March

2018; "I remember that *Songs From The Wood* was recorded in Morgan Studios, our last time there, and *Heavy Horses* was our first in the new Maison Rouge building, which we'd finished building in time to do the sessions."

Whilst it was clearly to Jethro Tull's advantage being able to make *Songs From The Wood* in England, it wasn't quite the same as having their own studio. Anderson told *National Rock Star* in February 1977; "It (*Songs From The Wood*) took a little bit longer than usual, became we did it all in England — the writing, the rehearsing and the recording. We were all living at home, which meant commuting in, and that obviously is time consuming. For me it was useful, though, because some of the songs were written on the train. It was quite fun to work that way. Obviously an album is best out when you're ready to do concerts. You do end up having a deadline, but it's a self-imposed one. In my case I impose the deadlines."

Of course, the Maison Rouge studio was for wider commercial purposes too. Anderson said; "It seemed quite important to me that it should stand alone as a commercial enterprise, therefore when we had people like Gus Dudgeon coming in taking seven days of work, then he got the priority and we would be standing there at midnight waiting for Gus to finish so we could get in and do a session from midnight to 6am."

As ever, Jethro Tull were a disciplined and focused band when it came to turning up at the studio and getting on with things straight away. Colin Leggett, who worked as an engineer at Maison Rouge, recalled: "The atmosphere for the *Heavy Horses* sessions was always good, although you were always on your toes for Tull sessions. They were always a 2pm start, and they usually finished by about 1am or 2am, never really late. Tull sessions were different from other bands. Some bands would take five hours to even get going, total lunacy, but Tull were always ready and on the ball."

It was maybe the case that *Heavy Horses* benefitted from the convenience of fewer distractions. For instance, regarding *Minstrel In The Gallery*, Anderson told *Beat Instrumental* in May 1978; "That was a very insular album as it was recorded abroad in the summer at Monte Carlo. A few members of the group decided that they wanted suntans and were conspicuously missing from some of the rehearsals. It's always a problem recording in an environment with a lot of recreational facilities, and you need a lot of willpower to stop drifting over to the badminton courts."

Regarding *Heavy Horses*, it was reported in the same feature in May 1978; "The processes by which these songs are transformed into group songs are varied, as Anderson explained. The relationship between him as the leader of the band and major songwriter and the rest of Jethro Tull has always been interesting."

To which Anderson was quoted; "It differs between every song. I try to avoid any formula for making music. I write a song and it remains as a voice and acoustic guitar thing until the other members add their contributions to it. At other times I go to them with an idea and it becomes a conventional backing track which they record for me to add bits over the top. In some places there will be an actual arrangement which I will give to members of the group, at other times they have complete freedom to come up with their own ideas. It varies between the members of the group being simply a backing band for me and me being just a singer with a group. They do write things as well — not a great deal, but what they do write is usually used."

Other bands to take advantage of what Maison Rouge had to offer were Gentle Giant, Genesis and Renaissance. Although by the late seventies, progressive rock was commercially on the wane in popularity, some fantastic albums were recorded at Maison Rouge. By the early eighties though, the studio began to cater for groups who were more pop than prog. 1980 saw a second smaller studio added on to the venue. Maison Rouge was proudly advertised as "simply two of the finest studios in Europe. Two twenty-four track studios, fully automated, bar and lounge."

Clearly happy with what the studio had to offer, the three Jethro Tull albums following *Heavy Horses* were recorded there: *Stormwatch* (1979), *A* (1980) and *The Broadsword And The Beast* (1982).

In 1983, Ian Anderson sold the studio to Robin Millar. Many memorable releases continued to be recorded there: *Fantastic* by Wham! (1983), Duran Duran's 'View To A Kill' single (1985) and Queen's 'One Vision' single (1987).

****

The opening track on *Heavy Horses*, '...And The Mouse Police Never Sleeps', was recorded in July 1977. Stylistically and lyrically it sets the tone for the rest of the album. It explores the cruelty of nature. The rhythm that appears at the beginning of the song was inspired by the drumming style of Artie Tripp who played for Captain Beefheart's Magic Band and Frank Zappa's The Mothers Of Invention.

Having released their album, *The Spotlight Kid*, Captain Beefheart's band had opened for Jethro Tull in 1972 during a tour of the US. On *The Spotlight Kid*, there is a track called 'Click Clack' where Tripp plays a groove rhythm. Anderson said of it in later years; "I kind of borrowed the backbeat weird syncopated strange rhythm. It's not exactly the same, but it's definitely got that rather odd, offbeat feel. Luckily, Barrie Barlow had cottoned on to that as well as he was in the band when we had Beefheart on tour with us in the USA."

At the time, such was Barlow's appreciation of Tripp's drumming that when he heard that Tripp had given up drumming to be a chiropractor, Barlow sent him a drum kit in the hopes of being able to persuade him otherwise.

It could be said that '...And The Mouse Police Never Sleeps' is more about a cat than it is about mice. The lyrics hone in on the savage nature of the hunt and the kill, and of how the cat is "licensed to mutilate". Whilst many of the songs on *Heavy Horses* are about animals, '...And The Mouse Police Never Sleeps' is certainly on the darker side of things.

Anderson told BBC Radio in March 1979; "I always have a soft spot for my cats, because I love cats, and I don't like cats that sort of... well what I do love about cats is cats that appear to just lie there and sleep and do nothing, but in fact they're extremely vicious, aggressive, nasty animals who tear heads off little mice and do all sorts of despicable things. And I call my cats at home — because they are salaried employees of mine, and they're there to keep mice away from the kitchen and kill rats and things, which they do; they find rats in the barn going after the horses' feet and that sort of thing: they dispatch them with all due alacrity, as David Palmer might say if he were here — I call them the 'mouse police'. That's my little name for them all, collectively; they're the mouse police, so I have a song called '...And The Mouse Police Never Sleeps', which is really about one of the cats in particular, called Mistletoe. '...And The Mouse Police Never Sleeps' is quite a good one."

"People always have this idea that nature is soft and sloppy and something even worse than hippies going on about love and peace, but it isn't at all. Nature is, I mean, most people can't face up to it — that's why we all live in towns and live in houses with central heating and want nice warm motorcars, because it's actually too tough for all of us. I'm just keen to point out that some of these things are a bit hairier than people imagine. Almost every morning I find some small, dismembered warm-blooded mammal. Mistletoe, he has a thing about the heads. He always eats the head and he crunches the skull and everything is gone, and he leaves the bottom half. Probably because it has the naughty parts and it puts him off a bit — his stomach turns just at that point — but he leaves these headless little furry mammals lying everywhere. That's pretty horrific stuff when you actually have to pick them up all over the place, and he brings them in, and the baby's in his pram, probably about to get a present from one of the cats — half a shrew, you know. So anyway it's all about that. It's actually quite a good song. I always say my songs are good songs, but this is actually a good one. It's well written, there's some nice lines in it."

David Palmer said of his contribution to the song: "I wrote what's called a fugue exposition based upon 'Three Blind Mice'. If you listened to John Evan and me on organ and various keyboards and you fish deep enough you can hear a short burst of 'Three Blind Mice' in there."

It was also in July 1977 that Jethro Tull recorded 'Moths'. The song's lyrics were inspired by John le Carré's novel, *The Naive And Sentimental Lover*. On the surface, it could be assumed from the title that the song is about insects but really, it is more about a game that features in the novel. Anderson explained; "It's a weird and tricky love story between three people, Shamus, Cassidy and Helen. Shamus the bad guy, is the seductive, crazy man, he's the dangerous sex, drugs and rock 'n' roll Ozzy Osbourne guy. And Moths is a game invented by le Carré, which Shamus plays with Cassidy and Helen, in which a candle is placed in the middle of a billiard table, and you score a point for each time you bounce the white ball off each side of the table around the candle."

Anderson told BBC Radio in March 1979; "It is your actual love song — that's what it's about, using the moths and the very transient affair that they will have around a naked lamp, or a candle in this case."

David Palmer's string arrangement on 'Moths' melds stunningly with Anderson's vocals and flute solos. Palmer said in later years; "What impressed me most of all in the course of recording the album was that Ian went into the studio with an acoustic guitar, and in two takes recorded 'Moths'. It's full of odd bar lengths, it's not like 1-2-3-4 repeated until you fall off the chair, it's very intricate. I watched him play the guitar and sing the song — twice. And one of those two takes is the master! It was stunning."

John Evan on harpsichord and the use of various key changes throughout a short song adds to the endearing folk flavour of 'Moths'.

Anderson said of *Heavy Horses* in later years that the title track was probably the first one he wrote for the album: "I can distinctly remember playing a G minor chord and it just rolled on from there. So that was a moment of exercising continuity from *Songs From The Wood*, because I was living in the same house in the same place, and getting a bit more involved in farming and other rural stuff."

At around nine minutes long, the title track offers a variety of musical ideas. David Palmer's orchestration (along with Darryl Way on violin) blends amazingly with Martin Barre's guitar parts. Orchestration and riffs together, the song feels like something that only Jethro Tull could do, especially in view of Anderson's lyrics and vocal delivery.

Anderson's voice sounds forceful and driven on 'Heavy Horses'. It drives the intense emotion of the song beautifully. However, there was perhaps a little more to it than that. He told *Prog* in March 2018; "I know some people have a lot of affection for the title track, but when I was recording that, I had a stinker of a cold and when I listen to the opening vocals in the quiet part of the song, I can hear the mucus and the congestion going on through my nose — it almost sounds like it was processed through something. Well, it was, in a way."

Heavy horses were used to carry heavy armour during wars. They were also used for transportations around rural areas and farms. Ironically perhaps, they were used by the original Jethro Tull (the man, not the band!); their strength was necessary for pulling his invention, the seed drill. At the beginning of the twentieth century, the use of motor vehicles resulted in a gradual decline in demand for heavy horses. The numbers continued to drop until by the nineteen sixties, there were only a few thousand of them left — remarkable considering that there was a time when they existed in the millions.

Anderson said, "There are very few breeders of heavy horses, and those breeds are now under serious threat of extinction because there are simply not enough mares and stallions left to do the business and not enough people to keep a horse that has no practical use in today's world. It's not a riding horse, or practically speaking, a draft horse any longer, in the sense that it's pulling a wagon. The interest has been falling away. There's a drive to try to save the breeds that are most under threat, because several breeds of heavy horses are traditional to our country."

Anderson told *Record Mirror* in May 1978; "Heavy horses are magnificent animals. It's impracticable to use them on farms these days because it's easier to fuel up a tractor and leap on the back. In manpower terms you've got to feed the horses and take a long time in mucking out the stables and preparing them for work. But of course to see them in a field pulling something is a wonderful feeling. But horses still have their uses, take the Highland pony for instance. It's used for deer stalking in places where wheeled vehicles just can't go."

He told *Classic Rock* in July 2015; "The title track of the 1978 album — it's about social realism, which is what a lot of my songs are about. I enjoy being observational, but also welcoming you into this world. Usually, I stick to subjects I know something about, although I have been known sometimes to stray into territory that's a little more unknown. But on this occasion I was sticking to my feelings about the changing world. The music was very much pastoral and British. It must have seemed like deeply unfashionable folk rock at the time, coming as it did towards the end of the punk era, and just before the next big thing happened, which was synth pop."

The emotion and the thematic obscurity in 'Heavy Horses' was such that at the time, Anderson drew parallels between that and the way in which international audiences may have responded to *A Passion Play*. Anderson told *Beat Instrumental* in May 1978; "I think that because *Passion Play* was rather abstracted both lyrically and musically, non English speaking people had to work that much harder to understand them, and having to do that makes them less likely to give up or take it for granted. That maybe accounts for its success in Europe. America's quite different, but they liked it too. It's just one of those things. I must stand by all the albums, I regard 'Heavy Horses' as the 'Aqualung' of this album. There's the same emotional thing at work there — feeling sorry for yet glorifying something."

He told BBC Radio in March 1979; "I have a soft spot for horses. I don't ride them: I don't like sitting on top of them, but I make friends with them and I have a few at home. Not that sort of horse, but I suppose it's rather like — I shouldn't be saying this, it's silly to say — but it's a bit like an equestrian Aqualung, if you like, where the downtrodden creature that I'm singing about is the poor old heavy horse who used to be in his heyday as the all-round working animal, both in industry and of course in agriculture. And very nearly disappeared altogether but for a few breeders who took a delight in preserving the species, and now it is beginning to come back again as a working animal."

"I wrote that one while we were in America, and it's one of the rather long ones. There are two long songs on the album, and that's one of them. It has a mixture of several different styles and a degree of ups and downs and level, what do they call it, dynamics or something. So that's the title track. One thing looking at the list of songs, now, is that they are all actually about something, which makes me happy, when I can actually see they are about something. The worst thing in the world is to find yourself writing a lyric which isn't really about anything at all; it's just an excuse for opening your mouth while the group make a funky, danceable, exciting, crowd-waving-their-arms sort of sound, which is pointless rock 'n' roll. Maybe some people would say it's not pointless and that it is in fact what rock 'n' roll is all about: unfortunately I do aspire to these higher pretensions and I must insist that it has to be about something. I mean Johnny Rotten sings about something, and in a very different way so do I."

After Jethro Tull had toured Australia to promote *Songs From The Wood* in 1977, they resumed recording for *Heavy Horses* in the October. It was during these sessions that two more songs were recorded: 'Weathercock' and 'Rover'. 'Rover' was written in dedication to Anderson's dog, Lupus, who had been immortalised on the cover of *Songs From The Wood*.

Anderson said of 'Rover' on BBC Radio in March 1979;

"It's about my dog Lupus, and I called it 'Rover' because dogs are reputedly called Rover, aren't they, either Rover or — what was the other one? — Fido! That sort of thing. But 'Fido' just didn't sound like it made it, you know. I couldn't hear Brian Matthew saying, 'Here's Jethro Tull with their new song, 'Fido''."

"But 'Rover' has a bit of romanticism to it, and it's really about my dog. He's running away, you see, and he has this basic desire to go out and copulate which he can't unfortunately do because we had a little amendment made to his, um, anatomy. We did that, unfortunately, because he did have this tendency to go off. He's a sheep dog, and given that livestock is nearby he will attempt to herd them, and is liable to be shot for his pains — interfering with other people's beasties. I get very angry when he does this, of course, really furious with him. He's brought back in disgrace, covered in mud and whatever else. But he does have that basic free-ranging spirit which I am attempting to acknowledge and in a tacit way applaud in this song. Although it doesn't sound like it's a song about a dog; it's sounds as if it's a song about Rod Stewart."

As the final track on the album, 'Weathercock' ends at the break of dawn. The simplicity is a calming end to an adventurous album in its use of acoustic guitar, mandolin and organ.

Setting off to tour the US again, it would be December 1977 before Jethro Tull were back in the studio to work on the final sessions for *Heavy Horses*. It was during these sessions that 'Acres Wild' was recorded. The song is a skilfully executed combination of folk instrumentation and rock music; it is strongly demonstrative of how willing Jethro Tull were to blend a range of musical influences. Anderson said; "As much as I enjoyed trying to play white man's middle-class blues in the sixties, it was my intention to try and find musical influences that, if they were the parallel to black American blues, would be in Europe. My inspiration comes from folk music, classical music, and of course I embraced church music. It just felt a little easier for me to develop my music along those lines, because I felt that I was drawing upon my own cultural roots and not stealing somebody else's."

When asked if he felt whether the inspiration behind 'Acres Wild' was "peculiarly British", Anderson said on BBC Radio in March 1979; "No, it's completely universal, absolutely. Absolutely. That's another thing: it would amuse me also to sing songs specifically about British institutions or situations. I think if they were at all critical, they would be, well I don't know. I just feel it would be a bit of a betrayal, in a sense: how could I really be so critical of it and still choose to live here."

In the same interview, Anderson also said that 'Acres Wild' is "talking about beautiful, desolate, rural, hard fantasy, but in the next verse goes on to talk about the city landscape as being another facet of the same thing. Which is really just setting off the two levels of desolation."

Darryl Way of Curved Air contributed the violin part on 'Acres Wild'. Curved Air had been an opening act for Jethro Tull several times in the early seventies. Way said of recording 'Acres Wild' and 'Heavy Horses'; "We did it in a single session, which was quite intense. What I remember most is how particular Ian was about what I was doing on those two songs and the amount of takes I had to do to get it exactly as he wanted it."

Thematically, 'No Lullaby' is a little different to most of the other songs on *Heavy Horses* in how there are no references to animals or rural life. Anderson, who wrote the song for his baby son James, explained; "I wrote this anti-lullaby which invites the child to stand up and face up to the demons and the bogeymen and the other scary things of the night — come out charging with rattle in hand."

He told BBC Radio in March 1979; "It always amuses me that whenever he (James) opens his mouth in the middle of the night he's descended upon by a flock of nannies and mothers and animals rushing to quieten him down and soothe him, whereas, in fact, you've got everything in the world to scream and shout about, everything in the world to be terrified about. So this is a sort of anti-lullaby saying, if you want to scream and shout and make a fuss then go ahead, because there's plenty to be frightened of. And in terms of the music it certainly isn't like a lullaby either — it's a fairly aggressive piece, so if I start playing that at him he'll definitely get no sleep."

The song is certainly an anti-lullaby in how it is more rousing than relaxing. Barriemore Barlow's drumming is tight and fast-paced and Martin Barre's electric guitar introduction is illuminating. Changes in intensity and time signature also serve to keep the listener on their toes.

'One Brown Mouse' is a straight-up folk rock song until in the mid-section, there is some effective orchestration from David Palmer. The song was inspired by Robert Burns' 1785 poem, *To A Mouse*. Anderson told BBC Radio in March 1979; "I've read very little of Burns' poetry, but I find him an interesting writer who was obviously a complete drunken lech, putting his heart into it. Just that particular theme appealed to me. I'm a very soft-hearted person when it comes to little animals, despite the fact that, blood sports and so on, is something that I certainly don't support, but if one includes in blood sports the killing of animals, as a sport, then obviously I do that to an extent, although, you know, I certainly don't approve of all of it. It depends on who's doing it; it depends on your personal motives and personal moralities. Despite the fact that I do kill animals, for food, and that's about the end of it, I do have a tremendously soft spot for some of them. And we're all just meddling about in that absurd balance of life and death which exists."

When Jethro Tull had started recording *Heavy Horses* in 1977, Martin Barre had only recently upgraded his guitars. For the album, he played Les Paul and Hamer guitars and used Marshall amps. His use of pedal is abundantly present on 'No Lullaby'.

The musical interplay between Anderson and Barre rings out impressively throughout *Heavy Horses*. There are many sections where their contributions weave together effectively before breaking off into solos that are played in sympathy with the songs (rather than merely on top of them). For instance, on '...And The Mouse Police Never Sleeps', Barre plays counterpoint to Anderson's flute. 'No Lullaby' is another instance in which the weaving of acoustic and electric guitars works wonderfully together; Barre uses volume for emotional effect and it is not the detriment of the quieter parts of the song.

Overall, the musical rapport between everyone in Jethro Tull was excellent during the making of *Heavy Horses*. Anderson told *Beat Instrumental* in May 1978; "One thing about all the members of Jethro Tull — and this includes past members — is that we're all rather odd musicians, unable to play with *other* musicians outside the band. None of us know the favourite standard rock 'n' roll songs that you can get up and jam, and this sets us apart from the mainstream. We are not versatile. John Evan can't even play rock 'n' roll piano to save his life. I can't play folk guitar. I can only play in five keys or something on the flute, so we do depend on each other as musicians pretty heavily. I mean, most of the band have only really played with Jethro Tull."

It's fascinating to think that the information revealed by Anderson in this instance is plausibly at odds with the way in which the music of Jethro Tull has inspired so much scholarly analysis over the years. There is possibly something to be said there in terms of taking music for what it is rather than delving so far into the theory of it that such study would inevitably go beyond what the musicians concerned may have intended or have even been aware of.

Once the recordings for *Heavy Horses* were complete, the band posed for a promotional photo in Anderson's home. Barre recalled, "Ian had got the cut glass out of his drinks cabinet and had run into the kitchen. We're all in there with our bowties, looking forward to a nice brandy or something to toast at the end of the album, and he brought in a bottle of Coca-Cola! The glasses in the photo are all full of Coke! I think that's what's known as Scottish brandy but I'm sure we celebrated somewhere else later."

The photo session for the album art was done over the course of one day. It seems like the handling of the two heavy horses required some patience. Anderson told *Prog* in March 2018; "I was holding on — they were very big! They were actually pussycats, those two horses — they were very good. The absurdity was that the shots that were taken were from a very long way away. It could have been so much easier. They wanted to get the valley in the background and the brow of the hill to give it some context, so I was a long way off. I had to walk an awful long way with these animals! The photographer was way over there somewhere — there was a lot of hollering and shouting. And you had to walk, and then it would be, 'Let's do that again, sorry!' But they were very well behaved. They were the best part of the day — they were nice animals."

Anderson said in the same interview; "If I'm honest, I wrote the songs as they came. It wasn't a concept album — I didn't really have an overall thematic approach. It really was a collection of songs, albeit with a certain sense of tone and mood, and at the end of it, *Heavy Horses* was the one that presented itself somehow. It had this significance and it was a visual reference for the album cover. And it was also, let's not pretend, quite a good title. That said, it's unashamedly about something that was lamenting the passing of an age. It's the equivalent of the end of the age of steam or when I do cathedral concerts at Christmas — it's celebrating what's possibly the end of our association with Christianity and the Anglican Church."

"Those things that you know aren't going to be around very much longer, they do exercise an attraction and an appeal, emotionally and intellectually, because you're having to chronicle something that you know other people are going to look back on and think, 'What on earth was all that about? I've no idea what they were'. And that was the kind of thing that was happening with those kinds of horses. Before we released the album, the band had a brush with some heavy horses in terms of pre-publicity, where we went to a brewery to see the dray horses there. They weren't using them as workhorses anymore — it was more of a showbiz thing. They kept a few as draft horses for taking the beer, so it was still something they were keeping alive for the tourists and for tradition, but it wasn't there for the daily deliveries anymore. So I'd met some heavy horses before, and though we (Anderson and his wife) didn't have heavy horses, we had a few horses around the place, so I was pretty comfortable being put in charge of those two monsters. That said, you have to remember that there had been various horses used in cultivation, but there were small, working horses, the pit ponies that pulled coal out of the ground. Working horses are not all necessarily of a larger stature, hence the album's dedication to 'indigenous working ponies and horses of Great Britain'."

The preface in the *Heavy Horses* sheet music book (the one published by Almo) states; "*Heavy Horses*, which has been certified as gold even before it was available, features the six-man team of Ian Anderson (vocals, acoustic guitar, flute), Martin Barre (electric guitar), John Evan and David Palmer (keyboards), John Glascock (bass) and Barriemore Barlow (drums). On first appraisal, one is immediately struck by the instrumentation and the theme — evident is a synthesis of each of the areas of rock that Tull have experimented with over the years — blues, folk, electric — and the overriding concern with the countryside, a subject which also spawned *Songs From The Wood*. The title track, 'Heavy Horses', is an affectionate tribute to Shire horses, now threatened with near extinction as machines push their way even further into the domain of the farm. Ian Anderson has been living in the country for the last few years, and after doing much of his writing in Holiday Inns and Boeing aircraft, he has now chosen his home as a base from which to draw the subject matter. One of the most diverse Tull albums to date, upbeat blues and rock tracks such as '...And The Mouse Police Never Sleeps' contrasts sharply with quieter ballads such as 'Moths'. *Heavy Horses* is indeed a beautiful collection, one that is sure to intrigue Tull fans on many levels, and a welcome addition to Jethro Tull's gold and platinum stable."

Heavy Horses was reviewed in the *Liverpool Echo* in April 1978; "Back to the land Tull go, maybe to discover their roots, who knows? What they have done is produce some beautiful songs as on 'Weathercock' and also 'Moths'. A very palatable platter indeed."

The same paper asserted in May 1978; "One of the outstanding tracks on Jethro Tull's new *Heavy Horses* album is 'Moths'. Ian Anderson is writing with a back-to-earth simplicity and this song is just right for these spring days."

The album was reviewed in *Billboard* in April 1978; "One of the most durable of rock bands, ten years as a group, Ian Anderson has not lost touch with the band's most appealing qualities. Finely woven together are blues, folk and rock elements which unite into distinctive pastoral-flavoured compositions. Anderson's identifiable vocals and flute are again at the forefront backed by Martin Barre on electric guitar, John Evan on piano and organ, Barriemore Barlow on drums, John Glascock on bass and David Palmer on the ever-present pipe organ. Anderson's central theme here is preservation of the countryside and nature, and by the way of textured arrangements and lyrical content, the message gets through." The review listed the best tracks as being '...And The Mouse Police Never Sleeps', 'Heavy Horses', 'Moths' and 'Rover' whilst calling the artwork an "attractive package for all those Tull fans to notice."

It was reviewed in *Cash Box* in the same month; "With *Heavy Horses*, Jethro Tull continues in the same genre as *Songs From The Wood*, mixing melodic ballads with heaviest rockers while the lyrics reflect group leader Ian Anderson's current fascination with the British countryside. The result is a beautiful lyric poem that evokes a completely different image in the listener's mind from most anything in the rock world these days. Should be heavy on AOR radio as well as at retail."

And in *Record World*; "Ian Anderson's concern for the country (a major influence on *Songs From The Wood*) is again predominant with a tribute to shire horses. One of the group's most eclectic LPs in some time, it is a synthesis of styles (from folk to rock) they have covered with much success over the past ten years."

And in *Record Mirror*; "Further rural ramblings from Ian

Anderson and co. Tull are getting so much into the mediaeval folksy bit that the heavy guitar noises in 'No Lullaby' sound totally out of place: an unwelcome (and anachronistic) intrusion. It's all very different from the crazed "progressive" outfit I used to know and love. In those days, Ian Anderson was the one-legged tramp in the filthy raincoat: these days he appears to be undergoing an identity crisis. On the front of the sleeve, he's the healthy peasant living off the land: on the back he's become the decadent lord of the manor. Very strange. The album meanwhile is dedicated to horses of all shapes, sizes and breeds — a nice idea, but we might ask ourselves what's it got to do with rock 'n' roll? Well, the answer to that is of course, not a lot — but no matter, I like it anyway. Though I must admit, musically, it's little more than a re-run of *Songs From The Wood*. I found it a totally charming collection of songs, but as with all sequels, the charm has worn off a little on the repeat showing. Still, there's enough here of interest to warrant a listen or two — try out 'Moths', 'Acres Wild' or 'Weathercock'. God knows what they'll do next though — a third album on the same lines definitely *would* be too much."

And in *Melody Maker*; "A long-time fan of Jethro Tull, I have recently become concerned by Ian Anderson's gradual decline. I'm painfully forced to compare Tull to an ageing dog: lots of bark but no bite. I remember praising *Minstrel In The Gallery* to the high heavens and remarking that after a rather bleak and unproductive period Tull were back on song again. Then came *Too Old To Rock 'n' Roll*, which was just a minor setback, and last year *Songs From The Wood*, a definite indication that Anderson wasn't interested in the uncompromising but still subtle rock that made the band renowned. And now comes *Heavy Horses*, and by its title alone you'd expect well, you know, a bit of rock 'n' roll. By rights, I should allow an artist of Anderson's calibre the option to move along whatever path he wishes."

"*Aqualung* is no more after all. It's finished, past and buried, so I suppose you've got to admire him for going on to fresh pastures, which is exactly what he has done. He has become obsessed with the countryside. *Heavy Horses* takes up where *Songs From The Wood* left off: a celebration of Mother Nature. An artist's music is a reflection of his surroundings, Philip Chevron tells me, and that is certainly the case here. Anderson has engulfed himself in the peace and quiet of his country home, his animals and his acres of land, and the result, not surprisingly, is music that is frequently timid and gentrified. Rock 'n' roll this ain't. That is a generalisation, and there are rare moments of inspiration on *Heavy Horses*; 'Acres Wild', 'No Lullaby', 'Journeyman' and the second segment of the title track which see Tull in a much better light, though most of them are touched by a gentle, folky mood that Anderson appears determined to maintain. This works sometimes, and Tull respond with a couple of beautifully orchestrated pieces, particularly on 'Acres Wild', 'Heavy Horses' and an otherwise wretched track, 'Rover', where the acoustics blend nicely."

"For those whose interest in Tull is confined to their raunchier aspects, there is but one track, 'No Lullaby', where Martin Barre is given his obligatory two minutes to get his guitar frustrations down on tape. It's an excellent track, powerfully aided by some funky drumming from Barrie Barlow. But what seems to make it successful is that the entire band have contributed and Anderson's influence does not hold sway. A pity the band didn't exercise the same resourcefulness on the rest of the album. But what makes *Heavy Horses* even more insignificant — I never thought I'd hear myself calling Jethro Tull insignificant — is the lyrical matter. A look over the track listing: '... And The Mouse Police Never Sleeps' (about cats); 'Rover' (a dog, although it could also be any manner of subjects) and 'Heavy Horses' (a hymn to horses and how one day they'll make a glorious return — the album is actually dedicated to a wide species of other 'indigenous working ponies and horses of Great Britain'). Anderson manages to break the deadlock only twice: on 'Journeyman', a sarcastic, witty observation of the commuter's daily travels, and 'No Lullaby', a rather frightening children's tale. The music is often quite endearing, but Tull's drabness is starting to frustrate me. *Heavy Horses*, with its log-fire, boy scout overtures, only compounds the felony. Of course, all of this will probably earn me a couple of nasty asides from Anderson on Tull's forthcoming British tour."

Heavy Horses was reviewed in the *Reading Evening Post* in May 1978; "This one has a conservation angle as Ian Anderson, the only original member left in the group, has devoted it to the heritage of the countryside, with a tribute to shire horses, which have been ousted from farms by machines. Composing the songs and producing the album, Anderson has obviously made *Heavy Horses* with feeling. It's a natural follow-up to *Songs From The Wood*, which also had a strong rural theme. The standard of musicianship here is very high, but then it ought to be. The ideas aren't so memorable though, and if you want to hear Tull at their best you'd be better off sifting through the racks to find *Stand Up* or *Thick As A Brick* than buying this one."

Rolling Stone reviewed it in September 1978; "The secret of Jethro Tull's longevity is that the band always plays its cards sparingly. For example, 'No Lullaby', one of *Heavy Horses*' two epics, deploys an extensive catalogue of aurally exciting effects: flanged drums, echo on the vocal, a mightily distorted guitar cadenza. But each item appears only momentarily, to nudge the slow dirge into grandeur. Another case in point is 'Acres Wild', a simple love song that's wrought entirely from the differences in timbre between Ian Anderson's mandolin and guest Darryl Way's electric fiddle. Similarly, Tull restrains its tonality to basic chord changes and folk-song melodies. But the rhythms are lavish — particularly the instrumental arrangements, where no two players are allowed the same part. *Heavy Horses* is merely the follow-up to last year's *Songs From The Wood*, which may well have been the group's best record ever. Anderson warns that this is the end of the folk-tinged Tull, that the band will return to boogie forthwith. That's a pity because this genre has suited Jethro Tull wonderfully."

It was considered in the *Sunday Times* in May 1978; "There is no denying the power, wit and freshness of Jethro Tull among British bands, they are almost unique — magnetic and magnificent after a decade of music making. They are however, almost too independently original for their own good. There is, through their many albums, a discernibly logical line in leader Ian Anderson's development as a composer. But the superficial twists in the band's career have sometimes left those who ride the bandwagon of pop taste — desperate to be thought in vogue — bewildered and insecure. Hence the spiteful attacks which greeted Anderson's *Passion Play* in 1973. Hence also the critical reserve in some quarters for his last album, *Songs From The Wood*, and his new one *Heavy Horses*."

"The infectious splendour of Tull's recent British concerts, the clamour of the audiences — how, at the Hammersmith Odeon, they rose to 'Heavy Horses' — and the riches revealed as the band play retrospectively, amply answer the grouches. Anderson, so much his own man, has leapt the generation charm, still winning young followers while retaining the old with his substantial repertoire of excellent contemporary music. He is, he's said, trying to fashion an English sound while still remaining a rock band. That, I think, does only scant justice to the magical mix of blues, folk, rock and jazz (listen, please, to his flute improvisations) which Tull pours forth. Yet the Englishness is unmistakeable. It emerges in his pastoral songs and acoustic gentleness. It's seen also brilliantly encapsulated in *Heavy Horses*."

"Anderson lives in the country, loves horses, would never be without them. 'Think what it's like to be cut off without petrol.' The song grew from that feeling, and from reading an article about Clydesdales while touring in America. There is feeling there, his emotions and his way of life outside entertainment reflected. Isn't that what good popular music is about — honest feeling springing from experiences? 'Heavy Horses' is a fine song glowing with evocative images. Yet Anderson's realist enough (his honesty is too fierce for some) to confess that Clydesdales can't cope with the agricultural development he's undertaken on his Skye farm — he has to use tractors. So, this is the enduring, enquiring, idiosyncratic, fascinating nature of Tull. Their concert performance reflects it. Bare stage, except for staccato lights mirroring the moods, as Anderson and his five splendid companions produce flute, guitar, percussion and keyboard solos and walls of sound fit to conquer. They do it all with a humorous, ripe theatricality, which, in its self-mimicking zaniness, is totally winning. David Palmer's mortician's stance at pipe organ, John Evans' impish obeisance to Harpo Marx, and the careful support of the other musicians to Anderson's gymnastic exuberance produce one of the world's peerless performances. Despite their longevity, Anderson and Tull have, I suspect, only just begun to surprise us."

Heavy Horses was the first Tull album to be released with the new blue label design. In some countries though (such as Mexico) the green label remained in use.

Some countries had their own unique label designs. The album was released on Chrysalis pretty much everywhere although Rhodesia (now Zimbabwe) and Turkey were two exceptions.

Columbia

Rhodesia

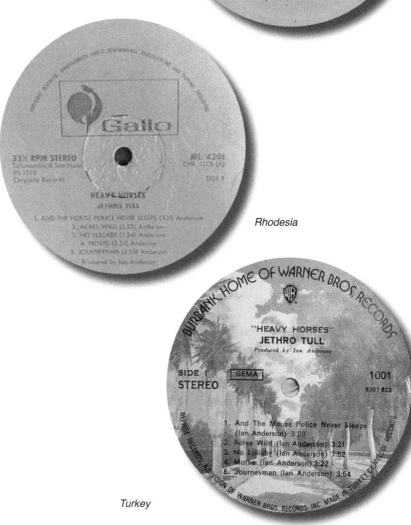

Turkey

Israel

Japan

There wasn't too much variation with the cover design. The Japanese released it with the usual obi — a paper sash wrapped around the cover to include information for the Japanese consumers.

In Uruguay the cover included the Chrysalis logo on the front but the back was vastly different.

The Argentinian release had the album title in Spanish.
A UK reissue replaced the green and gold for white and red.

Cassette covers

Australia

Venezuela

US

Yugoslavia

Greece

UK reissue

UK

Germany

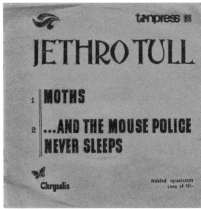

Poland

'Moths' was the chosen single backed with a non-album track. In Poland it had a different B-side and in France promo copies were pressed up with 'Acres Wild' as the B-side although on the commercial copies it was the non-album track, 'Life Is A Long Song'.

French promo

In 2018 the multi disc New Shoes box set was released. Amongst the five discs, a live recording from Berne is included.

Chapter Three

Bursting Out On Tour

The Heavy Horses tour covered venues in Europe and North America. The tour began in Edinburgh on 1st May 1978 and wrapped up on 17th November at Long Beach in California. It was considered in *Record Mirror* in May 1978; "Jethro Tull are ten years old and there's no wane in their popularity as they embark on another lengthy tour."

It was during the US leg of the tour that John Glascock had to take some time off due to health problems. Anderson's friend and former Stealers Wheel bassist, Tony Williams, filled in on bass. It had been reported in *The Birmingham Post* on 5th May 1978 that less than just twenty-four hours before they were due to appear, Jethro Tull had needed to cancel their appearance at Birmingham's Odeon Theatre. According to the report it was on account of doctor's orders due to John Glascock having sustained a hand injury. Of course, the details of this were kept brief and may or may not allude to the realities of the overall health struggles that Glascock may have been experiencing at the time.

In *Beat Instrumental* in May 1978, the interviewer concluded a feature with the consideration that "in London alone there are to be no less than five dates, and remember his (Anderson's) keenness; a) to keep performing however unnecessary it becomes financially; and b) that old perfection problem. A lot of people don't go for the lingering supergroups in this current climate, but Ian Anderson was smart enough, on his way out, to remind me that an awful lot of people still do. 'At least we go out there every year,' he stated, 'and we *deliver*'."

Anderson told *Record Mirror* in May 1978; "I'm not in it for the money anymore you know, my accountant might advise me to invest in a grocery business and make money that way. I'm touring because I enjoy it. Maybe it's true to say it's a feeling that gets in your blood. We've lost fans and gained them by the changes in our music so our audience are never just a sterile mass. It's always seemed to be a word of mouth thing with us. We've never had to rely on heavy press coverage. People would come to see us and tell their friends."

Jethro Tull's gigs the previous year had shown them as strong performers in the live arena. A gig that took place at Newcastle University was reviewed in *National Rock Star* in February 1977; "Ian Anderson walked on under a battery of ultra violets to massive applause. 'Here's a song my mother taught me,' was the brief introduction to 'Wond'ring Aloud'. The rest of the band took their places as required in the song's build-up. Newcomer David Palmer looked the part in concert pianist tie and tails. Anderson introduced him as 'trained at Trinity College of Music but saw the light.' The wit is sharp as ever. But his over-publicised sensitivity to press criticism after the *Passion Play* saga will become further mis-proportioned on this tour if his references to journalists continue to be as frequent as they were here. 'The next number is one from our new album which in spite of what you read in the press is marvellous,' was one of at least four such remarks during the night. 'Jack-In-The-Green' was the first of four cuts from *Songs From The Wood* that the band performed. The title track was followed by two medleys — a précis of *Thick As A Brick* side one and a superb sequence starting with Anderson offstage for an anonymous instrumental, returning for 'New Day

Yesterday' complete with classic Anderson flute solo — eyes popping, leg up, mucus flying and snatch breaths providing a rhythm. The hits kept on coming: 'Bourée', 'Living In The Past', more from *Thick As A Brick*. 'Aqualung' closed the set, but they came back to do 'Back Door Angels' and 'Wind-Up' and back yet again for 'Locomotive Breath'. You know how it feels: You come home on Cloud Nine after seeing one of your all-time fave bands, head straight for the LP pile itching to start the show all over again only to find the recorded article sounds positively tame. I knew I'd been to a good gig."

Long since the days of *Thick As A Brick* and *Passion Play*, by 1978, there was much less theatrical emphasis on Jethro Tull's live performances. Anderson told *Record Mirror* in May 1978; "I think we were the first band to talk to the audience. I mean we'd go on stage and laugh and clown around. After all these years it's still fun, but we haven't played the perfect gig, there have been many satisfying gigs but all the time we're still searching for perfection."

It was reported in *Beat Instrumental* in the May of that year; "As to the show the band will be taking on the road, the old favourites have been altered for the sake of change with faster tempos, different arrangements and instrumentals, a few of the new tracks have been added — although these will be quite different to the recorded versions — and the old theatrical tricks have been toned down."

To which Anderson was quoted; "We didn't want to become relied upon for that theatrical element. It is dangerous to the music in the long run. If it goes too far the music becomes the prop."

Regarding the setlist for 1978, Anderson told *Beat Instrumental*; "We've rearranged the show to place less reliance on certain old songs at key points in the show. 'Aqualung', 'Locomotive Breath', tracks like that have changed a great deal over the years."

Regarding the new material, Martin Barre told *Melody Maker* in May; "We had to re-learn the album, because after you've done a studio album it's such a relief of pressure you go away and forget about it. When you come back to play it on stage you have to re-learn your part. Psychologically you always feel under-rehearsed on tour, because of the pressure. The first shows are always nerve-wracking, but it's good in a way, for the adrenalin. That first show was unbelievable, so nerve-wracking. We were up in Scotland and couldn't believe we'd go out and play the thing right, without it all grinding to a halt. We change a lot of the instruments around from the album to stage, so there's a lot of re-learning anyway. We put one major instrumental bit into this show to feature the guitar and drums, when Ian wasn't on stage. We've done guitar and drum solos for years, but we wanted to change it for this show, and we just about got that right the day before the tour was due to start."

Chris Welch reported for *Melody Maker* in May 1978; "Last week in Berlin I saw the band play two hours with more energy than a brace of new-wavers for 7,000 fans who were still yelling for more, while the staff of the Deutschlandhalle were clocking off for the night... I enjoyed the concert even more than their recent Rainbow performance, although the acoustics of the Deutschlandhalle and the sheer size of the place made the band seem somewhat remote. Among the high spots were Martin Barre's beautifully constructed guitar solo on 'A New Day Yesterday', followed by Ian's surprise entry on flute which drew a roar of appreciation, and the guitar and drum outings on the unnamed instrumental sans Anderson."

"With songs from *Thick As A Brick* to *Heavy Horses*, the band performed a satisfying mixture of material old and new that adequately represented their ten-year output. As the strains of Eric Coates' 'Dam Busters March' boomed across the hall, I wondered somewhat nervously if the Germans might object to this hint of nationalism, but mercifully the tune seemed unknown to them, and certainly to the young Americans present, who have probably never heard of Guy Gibson, Barnes Wallis or the bouncing bomb. The band like to play the theme as giant balloons bounce over the audience, and the three unleashed in Berlin survived several minutes of pummelling before exploding in a shower of chalk dust. At least they weren't filled with water. There was a great thunder of feet as the fans demanded and got their encore."

By this point in Jethro Tull's tenure, it seems that Anderson took a pragmatic approach towards reviews. He was quoted in *Melody Maker* in May 1978; "If I read something that is adversely critical of what Jethro Tull is doing, I like to be told in a fair amount of detail why. If someone says, 'this is a load of rubbish', I like at least to have the option of profiting by somebody else's opinion and finding out *where* I may have gone wrong."

Besides, by 1978 Jethro Tull were very much an established group. Anderson told *Melody Maker*; "One of the reasons we don't have a support act on our tour is that we just can't find one that audiences will accept. I remember hearing 12,000 people booing Alex Harvey, who I like and had invited to tour with us. Of course he didn't help by telling them they were shit. It's happened to quite a few of the acts who have supported us. Captain Beefheart had a really hard time. But we only got our chance playing on shows with Yes and Led Zeppelin and I appreciated that."

"In the old days people wanted to hear all the groups. Now they only have the patience to hear the headliner. Livingstone Taylor came on stage to play one of our shows and had hardly played a single chord on his guitar before they were throwing bottles and cans and booing. Within thirty seconds he was hit on the head and knocked down and had to be carried off. He was in tears in the dressing room because they wouldn't listen to his music, and I was too. In a rage I promised him I'd go out and tell the audience what absolute bastards they were and rushed back to the stage. And when I stepped out — what happened? 23,000 people cheered me as if nothing had happened. What could I do or say? I just zipped up and played for them. But I didn't understand them. If we put on a support now, the audience would stay in the bar until we came on, and the poor group would have to play to a quarter-full house. I just can't explain the kids' behaviour. Livingstone Taylor was totally destroyed and I've never seen him again. If we were a new group supporting Led Zeppelin today, they'd probably do the same to us, and I find that very disappointing. How will new acts get their chance?"

Recordings of performances that took place on the European leg of the tour were released in September 1978 as a double live album, *Bursting Out*. It got to number seventeen in the UK and to number twenty-one in the US.

With their 1972 *Living In The Past* album accounted for where two of the songs on that are live ones, *Bursting Out* was Jethro Tull's first full live album. Phenomenal considering how long they had been going for by that point, especially seeing that they had often been keen to assert that they saw themselves as more of a live band overall. *Bursting Out* was recorded on an eight-track recorder. Anderson sold it after the album was finished.

In the newspaper advert for *Bursting Out*, Chrysalis described it: "For years now, Tull fans have cried out for a live album. It's here. And there's no question about it. This two-record set is the definitive "live" Tull album. Representing one entire uncut concert, the album clearly proves why

Ian Anderson is regarded as one of the world's premier performers."

Bursting Out was reviewed in *Record Mirror* in September 1978; "Why ten years on the road and fourteen albums had to go by before the release of a Jethro Tull live platter, totally eludes me. The more so since Tull are very much an on-stage group. *Bursting Out* was recorded on their recent European trek and features eighteen numbers including two new ones 'Quatrain' and 'Conundrum'. Classics like 'Too Old To Rock 'n' Roll: Too Young To Die', 'Thick As A Brick' and 'Minstrel In The Gallery' emerge with more force than in their studio versions. Ian Anderson's vocals are diamond-sharp and clear as a bell, matching the excellence of his flute playing. From Martin Barre comes invigorating guitar work, notably on the encore numbers 'Aqualung' and 'Locomotive Breath', while the rest of the band are in splendid form."

"The atmosphere is agreeably light-hearted, with some amusing remarks as Anderson introduces the material. Primarily what makes this album vastly superior to previous Tull works is the raw sound it attains, replacing the former complexities. Had the band released a live cut before, then maybe the "greatest hits" tag and the customary lengthy drum and flute solos of a double album, might have been avoided. Besides, single live albums are always more effective, and less heavy going. *Bursting Out* closes with a rendition of the 'Dam Busters March' more deadly than Sir Michael Redgrave's bouncing bombs in the RAF movie where it was first heard. With this riveting album, Jethro Tull are right on target."

It was reviewed in *Billboard* in October 1978; "One of rock's legendary bands finally has its first live album — a two pocket set and it's dandy. Recorded in Europe on a recent tour, the feeling is electric as the group reels dynamically over a long repertoire of material including well known hits such as

'Aqualung'. As ever the forceful and melodious flute of Ian Anderson is omnipresent over the basic rock instrumentation as tunes range from energised rockers to folk-tinged ditties. Anderson also provides witty introductions and narrative. Jethro Tull has been a consumer favourite for over ten years, with this package already shipping platinum."

And in the *Aberdeen Evening Express*; "After ten years on the road and fourteen studio albums, Jethro Tull have at last brought out a live double which superbly captures their dynamic stage act. Production by Tull leader Ian Anderson himself is near perfect — and this set should prove once and for all that although Anderson is the frontman of the group, Tull are no one-man band. This collection goes back to the early Jethro Tull, with 'Bourée' takes in the developing stages with 'Sweet Dream', has fan favourite 'Aqualung', the concept LP title track 'Thick As A Brick' and includes new folk orientated cuts such as 'Songs From The Wood' and 'One Brown Mouse' from the latest studio album, *Heavy Horses*. And it ends on a high note with the showstopper of rock showstoppers, 'Locomotive Breath'. Add to this the atmosphere of the crowd, the earthy humour of Anderson and the sheer all-round musicianship and *Bursting Out* is certainly one for the Tull fan — even if you have all the tracks on previous albums."

It was considered in *Circus* in November 1978; "*Bursting Out* bears convincing testimony. Drawing on material from 1969's *Stand Up* ('A New Day Yesterday') through 1978's *Heavy Horses*, Tull's first-ever live set is an animated documentary of their stage show, running the stylistic gamut from the quiet classicality of 'Bourée' to the heavy-metal huff and puff of 'Locomotive Breath' and the modal Scottish folk forms of 'No Lullaby' and 'Hunting Girl'. Anderson describes the album as 'a summation, a suitable point for saying 'this is it' to date. And it puts a little bit of pressure on us. It forces us into the next move'."

Prior to the release of *Bursting Out*, Anderson had told *Melody Maker* in May 1978; "It will be our first "live" album although there was a bit of "live" stuff on the *Living In The Past* album. This will be a double album of properly constructed music. It's interesting that it's not only our tenth anniversary but it's also one for Yes and Black Sabbath... There does seem a desperation for new music and new heroes, not only among the groups but in terms of those who document what goes on, i.e. the writers and critics. And those who have been part of the shaping of today's music must come under the heading of — what is it they call us? Boring old farts, or dinosaurs or whatever."

Across the entire first decade of their tenure, Jethro Tull were certainly a hardworking band. Anderson was quoted in *Melody Maker* in May 1978; "For ten years now I haven't had weekends off or a chance to go down to the pub for a drink or sit and watch the telly. We wouldn't have missed the success of the group obviously, but nearly all of us in the group can say we only have one friend apart from each other, which is pretty poor in terms of ten years of getting around meeting people. I have never really made any friendships within music. There are lots of people we know but somehow not the sort of people you would ring up if you had a night off."

Overall though, things were looking good. Anderson was quoted in the same feature; "Most people who know me and the rest of the group the longest, all say we have changed remarkably little and we are still here doing the same gigs! And that fills people with a kind of dread about what the real bitter truth is about why we do it. Either we are true showbiz professionals and say the show must go on, or else we must need the money, or else we are so locked up in our own little world we just go on doing it until we have heart attacks on stage. The truth of the matter is — we are always trying to do a better gig than we did last year. We change the arrangements — we still do old songs and we try new stuff. There is no-one more surprised than me that we are still doing this. Really. By the end of 1969 I felt I had done what I wanted to do and that was it. We played the world and had fairly impressive record success and I thought then: 'Well, that's it, there's nothing more to do'."

There certainly was though! *Melody Maker* reported in September 1978; "Tull To Reach 400 Million By Satellite: Jethro Tull are set to perform in front of the biggest rock audience ever when they play at New York's Madison Square Garden on Monday, October 9th. The 20,000 people in the stadium will be joined by an estimated 400 million around the world when the show is televised live by BBC's *Old Grey Whistle Test* and transmitted in stereo simultaneously on radio. Tull's gig is the first rock concert ever to be televised live from America and, as well as being seen in Britain, it is being broadcast to most of Europe, Australia, Brazil, and America itself. Other countries will show recordings of the concert. Each country's TV network is buying the broadcasting rights from Chrysalis, Tull's record company, who are producing the show."

"It goes out in Britain as an *Old Grey Whistle Test Special* on BBC Two at 11:15pm, at the same time as a radio broadcast as part of the *John Peel Show* on Radio One. It is repeated on BBC Two on October 14th at 5:55pm. The broadcast is a forty-five-minute excerpt from Tull's concert and will feature the band's best-known material. The Madison Square Garden concert is part of a six-week American tour by the group which starts on October 1st and includes four nights at the New York venue. To coincide with the tour, the band are releasing their first live album, a double called *Bursting Out*, due to be released on September 29th. Recorded during their recent European tour, it contains eighteen songs with a total playing time of an hour and a half. All the band's best-known songs are included as well as two new ones: 'Quatrain', written by guitarist Martin Barre, and 'Conundrum' by Barre and drummer Barriemore Barlow."

Melody Maker also reported in October; "On Monday night, Jethro Tull became the first rock group to appear live from America on British TV... Firecrackers and steel bolts nearly aborted an historic satellite broadcast. On Sunday night a lunatic minority pelted Ian Anderson with missiles during Jethro Tull's opening night at Madison Square Garden in New York. Anderson came off stage in a black rage and threatened to pull out of the transatlantic TV hook-up, ignoring the elaborate preparations and publicity build-up."

Anderson retorted; "If it happened again during the show, I would just have to say what I thought of the audience, and I don't want my parents to hear me swearing on TV. The tragedy is that most of the kids on Sunday didn't know what was happening and enjoyed the show. But I didn't think we played well and I was just miming to my own songs. I was being hit from above and behind by steel bolts and if people come supplied with missiles like that to hurt me, then I just feel like saying 'Fuck you, I'm taking the dollars and going'. And for me that is a complete betrayal of what Jethro Tull is all about. I actually do believe in those songs that I go out and sing, the songs from the albums mean a lot to me, and I want to give the best possible show and play the best music. But when this happens, just once in a while, then it destroys everything and I get really angry."

The report continued; "Sunday's show was virtually a dress-rehearsal for Monday night's telecast via the communications satellite, and necessitated the band preparing a new running order. A bad stage sound combined with the missile-throwing from fans behind the stage, and firecrackers from the auditorium, made the band tense and edgy. For the majority, the first show was a huge success; flaring gas lighters, thunderous applause and the obvious fanaticism of a 20,000 capacity crowd of new generation Tull freaks made it an impressive demonstration of the group's power and appeal after ten years on the road. But the tension and strain on Anderson was obvious, with the knowledge that an estimated potential audience of 400 million TV viewers would be seeing the band with every possibility of a serious incident on stage."

"Anderson is an intelligent, witty and sensitive man, whose family life is as important to him as his role as an eccentric rock hero, and he does not enjoy being set up as a target for crazies, who perhaps see him as a fairground freak and fair game for attack. In the event, the Monday — Columbus Day — concert and satellite transmission went off without a hitch. As the seconds ticked away in the control room at Madison Square Garden, the real stars of the hour, Tom Corcoran, BBC TV director of *The Old Grey Whistle Test* and his assistant, Rosa Rudnicka, kissed, lit cigarettes and emitted audible sighs of relief. The word came back from England — 'Sound and vision were great'."

"As *OGWT* producer Mike Appleton said, 'It was just like doing a show from the Odeon, Hammersmith.' The real significance of the whole exercise, nerves and tantrums aside, was that this could be the start of a whole new concept of rock promotion, where special shows are televised all around the world, helping to cut down the vast cost of touring. But even the Tull hook-up cost in the region of fifty-thousand dollars, with only the hope that losses will be recouped by selling video tapes of the show to other countries. Up until a few hours before the show it was being said that the COMSAT hook-up was going to be used to televise the show from New York live to Brazil, Australia, Poland, England and all points East. But it was eventually admitted that only England took the live pictures. Video copies were taken to be sent to Australia and even Russia, but it transpired that the expensive Chrysalis production was not being taken by the Eurovision network. Whatever the TV yields, it was fascinating to watch the twenty-four-hour build-up to the final forty-five minutes of live transmission. As a combined Anglo-American operation it worked as well as D-Day."

The satellite broadcast was reviewed in *New Musical Express* in October 1978; "If television has turned the world into a global village, then Ian Anderson of Jethro Tull clearly sees himself as the global squire. As he takes the stage for Tull's TV satellite show at Madison Square Garden, broadcast live last Monday to a potential audience of 400 million worldwide, there's no mistaking his patronising attitude to the assembled peasantry. Introducing a song called 'One Brown Mouse' before the televised segment of Tull's two-hour set, Anderson dedicates it to the Scottish poet Robbie Burns. This name-drop prompts a round of applause, as does every other utterance, and it's interesting to note Anderson's response. 'Oh, we've read him, have we?' he sneers. 'We are cultural, aren't we?' It's his tone of voice that's offensive, as much as what he says. Despite his Blackpool origins, Anderson these days affects the accent of a haughty British aristocrat. No doubt that's a major part of his appeal to young Americans, but it's ironic that Tull's concert programme boldly proclaims the location of their management company as the British Virgin Islands, a well-known tax haven. Clearly Anderson's upper-crust posturing does not extend to any very fervent patriotism. Arguably, his lordly pretensions would be innocent enough, except for evidence that he takes himself very seriously indeed."

"Reports are rife before the gig about Anderson's view of his own importance, and a wander backstage tends to support them. There is, for starters, the business about the dressing rooms. Anderson has his own dressing room and the rest of the band have a separate one. As it happens, both rooms are on a corridor that leads directly to the stage. Normally, it's the sort of thoroughfare that would bustle with activity. But when it comes to his privacy, Anderson is taking no chances. A burly Tull roadie bars the way. Anyone wanting to reach the stage must do so by a more circuitous route. So far does this isolation reach that the word is that Anderson rarely talks to his band, never mind the rock press. (Only the most conservative of British rock weeklies has been invited on the trip, with the remainder regally ignored). There is also the matter of the thermometers. These are attached to the monitors of the support act, Uriah Heep (no new wave bash, this one). The thermometers' purpose is to help with the tuning up. Anderson apparently insists that Tull's instruments are tuned at precisely the same temperature as that onstage, regardless of the fact that they'll have to be carried along a cooler corridor to get there. Obsessive? You might say so."

"Apart from basing himself in a tax haven, Anderson is also said to take extra care with other aspects of the band's finances. For example, while Tull leave their gigs in limos to impress the crowds, they actually arrive in cabs, which are obviously much cheaper. No wonder Anderson admires the canny Scots. With the current price of seafood, maybe he'll soon be swapping his codpiece for a fish finger. A careful deployment of resources is also evident during the gig. Understandably enough, Anderson saves the strongest material for the actual broadcast. As a result, during the thirty minutes or so before the gig goes live the gruel is very thin indeed. Convoluted, unmemorable melodies, topped off with pretentious, overblown lyrics. Interestingly enough, the much-maligned Uriah Heep provide a pointed contrast to the early stages of the Tull set. They play thirty minutes' worth of short, sharp rock songs, with a lot of emphasis on heavy guitar riffs and accessible choruses. A dinosaur fighting for survival, instead of simply dozing into oblivion. Happily, Heep eschew gimmicks, which is more than can be said for Tull."

"Ian Anderson is forever prancing around the stage like a geriatric ballerina — all spastic lurching and inelegance. He also has a very bizarre relationship with his flute. He tends to ram it into his crotch, and waggle it about suggestively, before sticking it into his mouth. Pretty weird, right? Maybe it's simply a matter of showmanship, doctor? Ah well, let's not be excessively dismissive of Tull's act. When it comes to the television millions, Anderson pretty well comes up with the goods, at least by his own standards. What the viewer at home gets is the very best of the Tull catalogue. The likes of 'Thick As A Brick', 'Songs From The Wood' and 'Aqualung' all come up together, as well as the set's strongest tunes, the 'Dam Busters March' and 'God Rest Ye Merry Gentlemen'. To be fair, 'Songs From The Wood' does provide a sublime moment, when the band muster a superb four part harmony, and drummer Barriemore Barlow springs up from behind his kit to provide a few notes of flute accompaniment. Anderson also turns out to have a nice way with adlibs. His ponderous flute solo is interrupted by a deafening, prolonged scream of feedback, and he comments: 'I thought the Russians had shot it (the satellite) down.' Maybe they should have."

"Ultimately, you can't help but feel that there's something a little sad about using one of the finest flowerings of technology as a device to plug Jethro Tull. There is after all something magical about the way a telecommunications satellite can transmit live pictures and sound around the world. To use it in this particular fashion reminds me of an old Dave Allen joke about an Irishman and a leprechaun. The leprechaun offers the Irishman three wishes, whatever he likes, and the Irishman says: 'Three pints of Guinness.' No doubt this analogy is unfair to Irishmen and Guinness, but you get the idea. One positive thing does emerge from this episode. The very notion of a global village is quite clearly exposed as absurd. The fact is that Jethro Tull were once a band who were much admired by their contemporaries in Britain. They're no longer respected in quite the same way at home, and their income depends predominantly on the compliance of American teenagers, many of them half the age of the musicians."

"There's something very disturbing about the wild delight with which old songs like 'Aqualung' are greeted. When that song was fresh, it was indeed very impressive. Nowadays, it seems to me to be no more than a relatively hallowed relic. If the world was truly a global village, then American kids would be turning on to the music of young British bands, not mouldy oldies from the sixties Evidently, America is lagging way behind Britain when it comes to the evolution of rock music. The spoon-fed adolescents there seem unable to think too much for themselves. The remarkable popularity of ageing bands like Tull seems to be a case of "Daddy knows best". The saddest moment of the entire gig came afterwards. A kid wandered drunkenly around the stadium, shouting 'Clapton is God!' You'd be hard pressed to find a more damning indictment of the state of American rock theology. Clapton may have been God once upon a time. But a lot of false idols have been smashed since then."

A disparaging review from *New Musical Express* but one very much in line with the genres of music that they were more in favour of championing at the time (punk and new wave in particular). Besides, even whilst they were slating Jethro Tull, there was still no getting past the fact that the band was incredibly popular with American audiences that year. It just goes to show though, that commercially, *Heavy Horses* was a risky album to make in view of the fact that simply in terms of genre, the likelihood of bad reviews (or indeed no coverage at all) from some areas of the music press was a strong possibility. Fortunately for Jethro Tull and their fans though, *New Musical Express* was not the Holy Grail and there were plenty of British fans anyway.

When *Bursting Out* was reviewed in the *Burton Observer & Chronicle* in October 1978, it was suggested that the large-scale broadcast would be excellent for the sales of Jethro Tull records: "It is hard to believe that *Bursting Out* is the first live album the band has made. Tull are one of the most popular live bands in the world and as there are so many live recordings on the market it seems high time that Tull was among them. The album, a double, is just what you would have expected complete with far too many verbal introductions and too much clapping and stomping. But at least Ian Anderson is fairly entertaining in his spiel and there are some genuinely exciting tracks among the onslaught of feedback and stage gimmicks. *Bursting Out* does manage to catch all the essential ingredients of Tull live and, after the recent Madison Square Garden extravaganza, there can be no doubt of sales prospect."

In November 1978, *Billboard* reviewed a performance that had taken place earlier that month at the Forum in Inglewood, California; "Tull's performance on 13th November (the first of two Forum shows) proved that the legendary English band is not too old to rock 'n' roll. Lead singer/flautist Ian Anderson appeared in better form than ever, stylising his stage antics through nearly fifteen tunes while pacing the group through a tight, just shy of ninety-minute set that included a fair amount of material from its landmark 1971 *Aqualung* album. While Anderson has toned down the length of the songs from the long excess, there were still a few spots where songs were overstated."

"Yet the band was so together that it made little difference. Nevertheless, Anderson is the focal point of the band. His limber gyrations and acrobatics gave him the appearance of a gymnast and the way he waved and spun his flute drew comparisons with a high school twirler. The first highpoint came early in the show with 1972's 'Thick As A Brick' which brought the surprisingly young crowd to its feet."

"Another that went over big was 'My God' (from *Aqualung*) which Anderson introduced and registered a loud roar from the original few notes. 'Songs From The Wood' was good but 'Heavy Horses' and 'One Brown Mouse' bordered on tedium. 'Too Old To Rock 'n' Roll: Too Young To Die' — which Anderson felt was misunderstood by critics as autobiographical — was greeted well. After 'Too Old To Rock 'n' Roll' Anderson departed the stage as guitarist Martin Barre led the group through a lengthy but tasty instrumental that concluded with a blazing drum solo by Barriemore Barlow. By solo's end Anderson had returned to the stage in time for the instrumental segue into another song from *Aqualung*, 'Cross-Eyed Mary', as Anderson sang and played flute through a strobe light. The band returned for two encores, both standouts. The first was 'Aqualung' followed by a blistering version of 'Locomotive Breath'.""

Chapter Four

A Legacy

Heavy Horses is held in high regard by not only fans of Jethro Tull, but the band themselves. As with all of their albums released up to that point (and indeed beyond), it is imaginative, original and a pleasure to listen to. It certainly has lots of replay value.

Martin Barre said in later years, "I think *Songs From The Wood* and *Heavy Horses* are two of the best albums from my time in Jethro Tull, Certainly from a songwriting point of view." He also spoke of how he considered his playing on those albums to be some of his best.

Anderson said, "*Songs From The Wood* and *Heavy Horses* were partners in an exploration of something that was not true to form in terms of either musical or lyrical content but it was "along the lines of" — in the same way that classical composers would often borrow from elements of folk music or other traditions that were fertile ground for developing their own music. But overall, I do think that *Songs From The Wood* and *Heavy Horses* encapsulate the element of folk-prog-rock. Yes, that's as good a way as any of describing *Heavy Horses* — it's one of Jethro Tull's folk-prog-rock albums!"

Amazingly, Anderson's immediate feelings on *Heavy Horses* after the album's release might not have been particularly positive. Not only was there a lot to do in terms of preparing for the tour, but there were also a few minor details on the album that didn't come out as he had been hoping for. It was reported in *Beat Instrumental* in May 1978; "Ian Anderson is not a happy man. Jethro Tull are to hit the road once again at the beginning of May and with just a few weeks to go he is becoming increasingly embroiled not only in rehearsals but in the heavy administration necessary to co-ordinate the whole operation. Breaking off rehearsals for an interview could only have compounded his displeasure at the arrival from town of the new *Heavy Horses* album cover."

Anderson responded; "There is always a great anticlimax when you finish an album and, like everything else, it has its shortcomings. In this case the front cover picture is wrong. It should be a square photograph, not a rectangular one, and I could have picked this out had I seen a proof. It annoys me that something should be less than right. There is also a slight distortion on the cut, a few little things which you wouldn't notice after fifty listens but that you do after one-hundred listens."

On balance though, he also told *Beat Instrumental*; "The sense of anticlimax when an album is finished is part of the recording process, as is the fact that I'm invariably writing for the next album by the time this one first becomes public property."

To say that *Heavy Horses* wasn't a step on from *Songs From The Wood* would certainly be flawed logic (that's not to say that one album is better than the other — they both stand up in their own right). *Heavy Horses* is demonstrative of a band that is very much on the same page working together objectively to explore new ideas, having already been in a good place with it all when having made *Songs From The Wood*.

Anderson said of *Heavy Horses* on BBC Radio in March 1979; "It's a rather more menacing sort of album; not menacing in the sense that it's a "downer" or negative, but a little more bite. I think the group are playing better on it as well. It's a cross-section of the ways that we record, which is a very important part of making an album. There are so many different ways you can make a record: you can rehearse a song absolutely note-perfect and then just go in and get it down, all playing, one vocal overdub and finished, or you can go into the studio with a vague idea and slowly build it up and add things and take things away, like an artist working with a painting, and arrive at the product that way — and it's the product of a lot of imagination, a lot of creativity, which is very spontaneous and which hasn't been rehearsed."

"Sometimes I go in and do just vocals and a guitar track and then leave the others to get on with adding things around it; or they go in and do something and I haven't even written the lyrics yet. Then I have the problem of working around something they've done. All this is, is trying to avoid using any kind of formula in making records — we try to apply all the different ways of making a record. Hopefully the songs have their own individuality and identity as a result of that variety of processes of recording. That is one of the reasons it has taken us a while, because obviously we tend to start work on certain songs in the studio and find out they're not going the right way and have to throw them out. I mean as usual we must have recorded twenty pieces, of which six or seven pieces on some tape lying around will never be dug out again, half-completed things."

The re-mastered edition of *Heavy Horses* released in 2003 includes two extra tracks — 'Living In These Hard Times' and 'Broadford Bazaar'. Thematically and musically, they both fit in well with the other tracks on *Heavy Horses*, so much so that it is surprising to think that they weren't included on the album the first time around. As a lot of Jethro Tull fans would probably agree, the bonus tracks that appear on later releases of albums often seem to indicate that the band had a wealth of material to choose from when it came to making most of their albums.

When asked if his songs about animals were saying something about society, Anderson told BBC Radio in March 1979; "Well, yes, I think there is, and that's what makes them valuable as songs: I'm not just singing about cats, I'm singing about something that translates into human terms, and in all the animals that I ever sing about there is something of a personification going on. I'm singing about people as well. That's what I think makes them good songs. They're not just literal. As I explain them they might sound a bit banal, and who knows, they may sound a bit like that when you hear them, but for me, if they're worth anything (at least as far as the lyrics are concerned) it's because they do have other shades of meaning, which is what makes them good."

After the success of *Heavy Horses* and the tour that followed it, for Anderson, the focus was already on making the next album. He told *Cash Box* in December 1978; "I don't like to listen to our earlier albums, because I'm already in the cycle of the next album and I don't want to break the cycles. Once the mixing is done I even have a great deal of difficulty listening to the test pressing. It becomes a painful process. Inevitably, one hears something that could have been done better. I prefer to leave the serious examination of my work to the people who buy it and listen to it. There's an essential difference between the performer and the audience and you can't pretend they're doing the same thing."

Heavy Horses was the last Jethro Tull studio album to feature John Glascock playing bass on every song. Glascock's health took a turn for the worst during the making of *Stormwatch*. New York's *Daily News* reported in October 1979 "Tull was stopped cold in the recording studio last year when bassist John Glascock had to quit the band after unsuccessful heart surgery. *Stormwatch* was only halfway completed at the time." Glascock passed away at the age of twenty-eight as a result of a congenital heart valve defect.

In the grand scheme of Jethro Tull's tenure, there was much more to come after *Heavy Horses*. Anderson had every desire to keep going, and not just for commercial reasons. He was quoted in *Billboard* in November 1978; "I don't see any reason why we should have to stop performing. We'll go on doing it as long as we continue to enjoy it. I wouldn't pretend that we will be out on the road ten months out of the year but certainly a minimum amount of touring is required to keep you physically and mentally attuned to the music you are doing in the studio. You have to perform to real people in addition to making records. We will tour with the frequency we are doing now, approximately four or five months out of the year, worldwide... Apart from the fact that our music has had some lasting value for some people, I think importantly to that is that we are not relying on overt commerciality or overt exploitation. You haven't heard about Jethro Tull being involved in drug scandals. The thing that keeps us going is that we have audiences all over the world telling each other about Jethro Tull. They don't rely on the daily papers, TV talk shows or top forty radio to tell them about us."

Anderson told *Cash Box* in December 1978; "I want to continue to make music. Sometimes the process is fun, sometimes it's painful, but as a kind of work it is intuitively exciting, sort of creative on a lofty plane. I don't feel I've done it yet as well as I can and I feel I have a lot left to give, so I'm going to keep doing it... One of the sad things about my job is that in spite of the artistry to which one might subscribe, it does come back to using the same words in terms of selling the product as are applicable in any other industry, such as packaging and merchandising and "the industry" as it's referred to. I cringe in embarrassment when I hear people talk about "the industry". Our business has a special flair that shouldn't be lost in the trite business aspects. I see many people who had the flair, that special creativity, who now have become concerned about maintaining that position as part of "the industry"."

He told *Record Mirror* in May 1978; "Jethro Tull music has always been very eclectic, we never set out to be deliberately commercial. If I listen to the charts today then it seems that a lot of singles are just derivative of all the other singles. I prefer something that will stimulate and educate me. The feeling seems to me that if you're going to make it then you've got to wear a certain pair of ex-army trousers and look like everybody else. The media is really using its power to force people into that situation."

The plan was actually to make a very different-sounding album after *Heavy Horses*. In June 1978, Anderson was quoted in *Billboard* as having said that *Heavy Horses* marks the "end of Tull's juggling with softer material and the rock idiom. In the future we will be recording more rock-oriented albums, works that are more dynamic, more aggressive and show the band capable of playing heavier pieces of music." Of course, the following album, *Stormwatch* (1979) still has the distinctive sound of Jethro Tull that features on *Heavy Horses*; the blend of folk influences certainly remains. Whether or not *Stormwatch* is actually "heavier" than *Heavy Horses* is certainly debateable but either way, Jethro Tull's 1979 album would certainly put forward a whole host of new ideas and themes.

The title track on *Heavy Horses* has long been played in live sets. It has been changed a little in recent years though.

Anderson told *Prog* in March 2018; "I changed it a few years ago, to bring some other elements into it. I changed some of the lyrics, which is a brave and perhaps silly thing to do, but I wanted to give a little bit more emphasis to put in context that world — I guess, being over thirty years later, it's even less likely to encounter working horses. In fact, right at this moment, there's a lot of pressure on the gene pool for a lot of rare breeds of horses, so it's looking a bit rough for some of them as there are fewer people willing to look after them and so forth. The problem is that they're not riding horses — you can't hop on their back and go for a walk; they don't race. They're just an impediment, really, in terms of the fact that they need a lot of land to graze and need to be mucked out and looked after just like any other horse. It's not their fault, but they can't earn their living these days."

"So I thought it'd be nice just to bring in the context, so the second verse now starts with a reference to 'nothing runs like a Deere', which is the slogan for the famous John Deere tractors. I'm trying to make the more obvious comparison with today's world where we talk in terms of horsepower, but today's world is full of air-conditioned cabs and hydraulic seats and suspension. It's a very different world, which was just beginning to happen when I got into farming. You know, I think there's something to be said for people getting their hands dirty. And I think, in a way, there's something more romantic and, dare I say it, something more satisfying at the end of the day about humping bales of hay than humping Marshall cabinets into the back of a transit van. And you get cold and sore hands, but it's good for the soul and it's all tied in with that thing that along the way, and over the years, you've done something, be it farming or whatever. But the one thing is that you have to be prepared to get down and dirty and get wet and cold, get back to the earth, to a more traditional way of doing things."

March 2018 saw the release of a five-disc fortieth anniversary version of *Heavy Horses*. Featured on it are alternative takes and outtakes, previously unreleased live tracks and detailed annotations from Ian Anderson.

A stand-out album between *Songs From The Wood* and *Stormwatch* (and indeed, from Jethro Tull's discography overall), *Heavy Horses* is a wonderful blend of folk and rock. With memorable lyrics and melodies, and innovative use of instrumentation, it kept Jethro Tull firmly in the limelight in 1978. Whilst *Stormwatch* would see the band start to take off in a new direction that ultimately led to them embracing a somewhat different sound for the early eighties, *Heavy Horses* shows Jethro Tull at a commercial and creative peak. With stories of sweet mice, brutal cats and hardworking horses, it is full of textures and ideas that bring something of interest with every spin on the turntable. With precise production and songs that have facilitated strong live performances, the album is important not only for Jethro Tull and their legacy, but for fans who will knowingly find much joy in giving the album yet another play.

Discography

Personnel

Jethro Tull

Ian Anderson – lead vocals, flute, acoustic guitar, additional electric guitar, mandolin
Martin Barre – electric guitar
John Glascock – backing vocals, bass guitar
John Evan – piano, organ
David Palmer – keyboards, portative pipe organ, orchestral arrangements
Barriemore Barlow – drums, percussion

Additional personnel

Darryl Way – violin (on 'Acres Wild' and 'Heavy Horses')
Shona Anderson – photography
Robin Black – sound engineer
James Cotier – photography

JETHRO TULL: Moths (Chrysalis CHS 2214). More pop-orientated and deliberately lightweight than most of his stuff, I s'pose, this sounds to me like a cross between Cat Stevens, Neil Diamond and the current Genesis single. But then I'm no judge: I've never been able to fathom Ian Anderson's arcane meanderings.

Time Signatures

...And The Mouse Police Never Sleeps
3/4 throughout.

Acres Wild
2/2 throughout.

No Lullaby
3/4 until 4/4 at "come out fighting..."

Moths
*Starts with phrases in two bars of 3/4 plus one bar of 2/4
*After "chasing shadows slipping in" it remains in 4/4 up to and including "on a night light ride"
*Ditto "golden needle's eye" through to "lemming said"
*Ditto "candle burned" through to first "suicidal came"
*"Suicidal came, came to join in worship" covers four bars of 3/4 and one bar of 2/4 before the rest of the song remains in 4/4.

Journeyman
The section of "to each journeyman his own..." through to "on the late commuter special" is in 4/4 throughout. In all other instances, phrases are a combination of bars in 2/4, 3/4 and 4/4.

Rover
*Starts with phrases in two bars of 3/4 plus one bar of 2/4
*From "call the tune I'm ready" onwards, phrases are a combination of bars in 2/4, 3/4 and 4/4.

One Brown Mouse
4/4 throughout except for one bar of 2/4 then five bars of 3/4 for the intro.

Heavy Horses
*Starts off in 4/4 but then many phrases cover varying numbers of bars in 4/4 with a 2/4 bar at the end.
*Single bars of 3/4 occur in some places (e.g. "cold winds fac –" and "low sun rac –").

Weathercock
4/4 throughout.

Track Listing

All tracks are written by Ian Anderson with additional material by Martin Barre and David Palmer.

Side One
1. ...And The Mouse Police Never Sleeps (3:11)
2. Acres Wild (3:22)
3. No Lullaby (7:55)
4. Moths (3:24)
5. Journeyman (3:55)

Side Two
6. Rover (The 2003 re-mastered CD includes an alternate mix of the track) (4:17)
7. One Brown Mouse (3:21)
8. Heavy Horses (8:58)
9. Weathercock (4:02)

2003 Bonus Tracks
10. Living In These Hard Times (3:10)
11. Broadford Bazaar (3:38)

2018 40th Anniversary New Shoes Deluxe Edition

In March 2018, Jethro Tull released a five disc "bookset" version of *Heavy Horses*. It included a ninety-six-page booklet with annotations by Ian Anderson; track-by-track and regarding associated recordings. It is similar to the band's other fortieth anniversary reissues whereby the first disc features Steven Wilson's stereo remixes followed by associated recordings of seven previously unreleased tracks. The second and third discs contain twenty-two previously unreleased live tracks — they were recorded on 28th May 1978 at the Festhalle in Berne Switzerland during the European leg of the Heavy Horses tour. The previously unreleased tracks were remixed to stereo by King Crimson's Jakko Jakszyk. The set also includes DVDs.

CD One: Steven Wilson stereo remix of the album and associated recordings
1. ...And The Mouse Police Never Sleeps
2. Acres Wild
3. No Lullaby
4. Moths
5. Journeyman
6. Rover
7. One Brown Mouse
8. Heavy Horses
9. Weathercock
10. Living In These Hard Times (version 2, previously unreleased)
11. Everything In Our Lives (previously unreleased)
12. Jack A Lynn (early version, previously unreleased)
13. Quatrain (studio version, previously unreleased)
14. Horse-Hoeing Husbandry (previously unreleased)
15. Beltane
16. Botanic Man (previously unreleased)
17. Living In These Hard Times (version 1)
18. Botanic Man Theme (previously unreleased)

CD Two: Live in Concert: Berne, Switzerland, May 1978, Jakko Jakszyk stereo mix
1. Opening Music (Quartet)
2. Intro By Claude Nobs
3. No Lullaby
4. Sweet Dream
5. Skating Away On The Thin Ice Of The New Day
6. Jack-In-The-Green
7. One Brown Mouse
8. Heavy Horses
9. A New Day Yesterday
10. Flute Solo Improvisation/God Rest Ye Gentlemen/Bourée
11. Living In The Past/A New Day Yesterday (reprise)
12. Songs From The Wood

CD Three: Live in Concert: Berne, Switzerland, May 1978, Jakko Jakszyk stereo mix
1. Thick As A Brick
2. Hunting Girl
3. Too Old To Rock 'n' Roll: Too Young To Die
4. Conundrum
5. Minstrel In The Gallery
6. Cross-Eyed Mary
7. Quatrain
8. Aqualung
9. Locomotive Breath
10. Dam Busters March/Aqualung (Reprise)

DVD One: Steven Wilson 5.1 surround and stereo mixes and flat transfer of the original stereo and quadraphonic mixes of the album and selected associated recordings

1. ...And The Mouse Police Never Sleeps (Steven Wilson DD/DTS 5.1 Surround Remix)
2. Acres Wild (Steven Wilson DD/DTS 5.1 Surround Remix)
3. No Lullaby (Steven Wilson DD/DTS 5.1 Surround Remix)
4. Moths (Steven Wilson DD/DTS 5.1 Surround Remix)
5. Journeyman (Steven Wilson DD/DTS 5.1 Surround Remix)
6. Rover (Steven Wilson DD/DTS 5.1 Surround Remix)
7. One Brown Mouse (Steven Wilson DD/DTS 5.1 Surround Remix)
8. Heavy Horses (Steven Wilson DD/DTS 5.1 Surround Remix)
9. Weathercock (Steven Wilson DD/DTS 5.1 Surround Remix)
10. Living In These Hard Times (version 2, previously unreleased) (Steven Wilson DD/DTS 5.1 Surround Remix)
11. Everything In Our Lives (previously unreleased) (Steven Wilson DD/DTS 5.1 Surround Remix)
12. Jack A Lynn (early version, previously unreleased) (Steven Wilson DD/DTS 5.1 Surround Remix)
13. Horse-Hoeing Husbandry (previously unreleased) (Steven Wilson DD/DTS 5.1 Surround Remix)
14. Beltane (Steven Wilson DD/DTS 5.1 Surround Remix)
15. Botanic Man (previously unreleased) (Steven Wilson DD/DTS 5.1 Surround Remix)
16. Living In These Hard Times (version 1) (Steven Wilson DD/DTS 5.1 Surround Remix)
17. Botanic Man Theme (previously unreleased) (Steven Wilson DD/DTS 5.1 Surround Remix)
18. A Town In England (Steven Wilson DD/DTS 5.1 Surround Remix)
19. ...And The Mouse Police Never Sleeps (Steven Wilson Remix in 96/24 PCM Stereo)
20. Acres Wild (Steven Wilson Remix in 96/24 PCM Stereo)
21. No Lullaby (Steven Wilson Remix in 96/24 PCM Stereo)
22. Moths (Cap In Hand) (Steven Wilson Remix in 96/24 PCM Stereo)
23. Journeyman (Steven Wilson Remix in 96/24 PCM Stereo)
24. Rover (Steven Wilson Remix in 96/24 PCM Stereo)
25. One Brown Mouse (Steven Wilson Remix in 96/24 PCM Stereo)
26. Heavy Horses (Steven Wilson Remix in 96/24 PCM Stereo)
27. Weathercock (unedited master) (Steven Wilson Remix in 96/24 PCM Stereo)

28. Living In These Hard Times (version 2, previously unreleased) (Steven Wilson Remix in 96/24 PCM Stereo)

29. Everything In Our Lives (previously unreleased) (Steven Wilson Remix in 96/24 PCM Stereo)

30. Jack A Lynn (early version, previously unreleased) (Steven Wilson Remix in 96/24 PCM Stereo)

31. Quatrain (studio version, previously unreleased) (Steven Wilson Remix in 96/24 PCM Stereo)

32. Horse-Hoeing Husbandry (previously unreleased) (Steven Wilson Remix in 96/24 PCM Stereo)

33. Beltane (Steven Wilson Remix in 96/24 PCM Stereo)

34. Botanic Man (previously Unreleased) (Steven Wilson Remix in 96/24 PCM Stereo)

35. Living In These Hard Times (version 1) (Steven Wilson Remix in 96/24 PCM Stereo)

36. Botanic Man Theme (previously unreleased) (Steven Wilson Remix in 96/24 PCM Stereo)

37. A Town In England (Steven Wilson Remix in 96/24 PCM Stereo)

38. ...And The Mouse Police Never Sleeps (96/24 PCM Flat Transfer – Original Stereo Master)

39. Acres Wild (96/24 PCM Flat Transfer – Original Stereo Master)

40. No Lullaby (96/24 PCM Flat Transfer – Original Stereo Master)

41. Moths (96/24 PCM Flat Transfer – Original Stereo Master)

42. Journeyman (96/24 PCM Flat Transfer – Original Stereo Master)

43. Rover (96/24 PCM Flat Transfer – Original Stereo Master)

44. One Brown Mouse (96/24 PCM Flat Transfer – Original Stereo Master)

45. Heavy Horses (96/24 PCM Flat Transfer – Original Stereo Master)

46. Weathercock (96/24 PCM Flat Transfer – Original Stereo Master)

47. Rover (No Strings Version) (Flat Transfer)

48. Living In These Hard Times (Version 2) (Flat Transfer)

49. Beltane (Flat Transfer)

DVD Two: recorded live to 24 track at The Festhalle, Berne, Switzerland by The Maison Rouge Mobile mixed to 5.1 DTS & DD surround sound and 48/24 LPCM stereo (tracks 1-22) and 96/24 stereo (tracks 23-44) by Jakko Jakszyk.

1. Opening Music (Quartet)
2. Introduction By Claude Nobs
3. No Lullaby
4. Sweet Dream
5. Skating Away On The Thin Ice Of The New Day
6. Jack-In-The-Green
7. One Brown Mouse
8. Heavy Horses
9. A New Day Yesterday
10. Flute Solo Improvisation/God Rest Ye Gentlemen/Bourée
11. Living In The Past/ A New Day Yesterday (reprise)
12. Songs From The Wood
13. Thick As A Brick
14. Hunting Girl
15. Too Old To Rock 'n' Roll: Too Young To Die
16. Conundrum
17. Minstrel In The Gallery
18. Cross-Eyed Mary
19. Quatrain
20. Aqualung
21. Locomotive Breath
22. Dam Busters March/Aqualung (Reprise)
45. Heavy Horses (Video)
46. Moths (Video)
47. Bursting Out (TV Advertisement) (Video)
48. Bursting Out and Madison Square Garden show (TV Advertisement) (Video)

Original April 1978 UK releases:
Chrysalis CHR 1175, LP
Chrysalis ZCHR 1175, cassette

Reissues:
Chrysalis CCD 1175, CD
Chrysalis CHR 1175, LP, 1989*
*With white / red cover.

Chrysalis CDP 32 1175 2, CD
Chrysalis – 7243 5 81571 2 3, CD, 2003*
*Remastered with two bonus tracks.

Chrysalis 0190295757915, 5 discs, 2018
(New Shoes Edition)

Chrysalis 0190295757311 LP, April 20th 2018

Original April 1978 US releases:
Chrysalis CHR 1175, LP
Chrysalis CCH 1175, cassette
Chrysalis 8CH 1175, 8-track
Chrysalis 1R1 6790, Reel

Reissues:
Chrysalis   PV 41175 LP
Chrysalis   PVT 41175 cassette
Chrysalis   VK 41175 CD
Chrysalis   F2 21175 CD 1994
Chrysalis   72435-81571-2-3 CD 2003*
*Remastered with two bonus tracks

Moths / Life Is A Long Song
Chrysalis CHS 2214, UK, March 1978

This was initially pressed up with a different B-side — 'Beltane' but it was withdrawn in favour of a different non-album track. Irish copies leaked onto the market with 'Beltane' listed on the B-side although the record actually played 'Life Is A Long Song'. Couplings of this release are also known to have been released in Australia, New Zealand, Germany and France. Rare promotional copies from France had a different B-side however; 'Acres Wild'.

Moths / ...And The Mouse Police Never Sleeps
Tonpress S-166, Poland

Unique coupling released on Poland's state-owned label.

Reissues:
Moths 10" EP
Chrysalis 0190295730413, 21st April 2018

The tracks are: Moths (Steven Wilson Remix) / Living In These Hard Times (Version 2 Original Mix) /
Life Is A Long Song / Beltane (Original Mix) / A Stitch In Time (Full Version) / Sweet Dream (Live) //

Jethro's 'Horse' play

JETHRO TULL have now confirmed the dates for their May tour of Britain, which follows the release of their new album, 'Heavy Horses', by Chrysalis on April 1.

The band will open at Edinburgh Usher Hall on May 1 and then play Glasgow Apollo 2, Manchester Apollo 3-4, Birmingham Odeon 5, London Rainbow 7-8, London Hammersmith Odeon 9-10. More dates may be added later.

Tickets are priced at £3.50, £2.75 and £2.00 outside London and £4.00, £3.25 and £2.50 at the Rainbow and Hammersmith Odeon.

Tull will be playing the show with no support act and the British dates are the beginning of a 'Heavy Horses World Trek' which will occupy them for the rest of the year.

Tour Dates

1977

14th January	Pasadena Civic Auditorium, Pasadena, USA
15th January	Pasadena Civic Auditorium, Pasadena, USA
16th January	Dorothy Chandler Pavilion, LA, USA
19th January	Masonic Auditorium, Detroit, USA
20th January	Masonic Auditorium, Detroit, USA
22nd January	Radio City Music Hall, New York, USA
23rd January	Radio City Music Hall, New York, USA
1st February	Capitol Theatre, Aberdeen, UK
2nd February	Apollo Theatre, Glasgow, UK
3rd February	City Hall, Newcastle, UK
4th February	Apollo, Manchester, UK
5th February	Apollo, Manchester, UK
6th February	Odeon, Birmingham, UK
7th February	Empire Theatre, Liverpool, UK
9th February	Gaumont Theatre, Southampton, UK
11th February	Hammersmith Odeon, London, UK
12th February	Hammersmith Odeon, London, UK
13th February	Hammersmith Odeon, London, UK
14th February	Colston Hall, Bristol, UK
23rd February	Sports Arena, San Diego, USA (cancelled but rescheduled for 8th April)
25th February	Anaheim Convention Centre, Anaheim, USA
1st March	Oakland Coliseum, Oakland, USA
3rd March	Seattle Coliseum, Seattle, USA
4th March	University Of Oregon, Eugene, USA
5th March	Washington State University, Pullman, USA
6th March	University Of Montana, Missoula, USA
8th March	McNichols Arena, Denver, USA
9th March	Omaha City Auditorium Arena, Omaha, USA

10th March	University Of Missouri, Columbia, USA
11th March	Riverfront Coliseum, Cincinnati, USA
12th March	North Western Illinois University, Evanston, USA
13th March	Kiel Auditorium, St Louis, USA
14th March	Municipal Auditorium, Nashville, USA
15th March	Mid-South Coliseum, Memphis, USA
16th March	Louisville Gardens Convention Centre, Louisville, USA
17th March	Chicago Stadium, Chicago, USA
18th March	Bradley University Field House, Peoria, USA
19th March	St John's Arena, Colombo, USA
21st March	Cobo Hall, Detroit, USA
22nd March	Cobo Hall, Detroit, USA
23rd March	Richfield Coliseum, Cleveland, USA
24th March	Maple Leaf Gardens, Toronto, Canada

| 25th March | Montreal Forum, Montreal, Canada |
| 26th March | Ottawa Civic Centre, Ottawa, Canada |

28th March	Boston Tea Gardens, Boston, USA
29th March	Buffalo War Memorial Auditorium, Buffalo, USA
30th March	Syracuse War Memorial, Syracuse, USA
31st March	Veterans Memorial Coliseum, New Haven, USA

1st April	Veterans Memorial Coliseum, New Haven, USA
6th April	Anaheim Convention Centre, Anaheim, USA
7th April	Anaheim Convention Centre, Anaheim, USA
8th April	Sports Arena, San Diego, USA
9th April	Long Beach Arena, Long Beach, USA
10th April	Aladdin Theatre, Las Vegas, USA
16th April	Messecentrum, Nurnberg, Germany
17th April	Olympiahalle, Munich, Germany
18th April	Festhalle, Frankfurt, Germany
19th April	Eilenfriedehalle, Hannover, Germany
20th April	Sporthalle, Collogne, Germany
21st April	Grugahalle, Essen, Germany
22nd April	Stadthalle, Bremen, Germany
23rd April	Deutschlandhalle, Berlin, Germany

24th May	Konserthuset, Stockholm, Sweden
25th May	Scandinavium, Gothenburg, Sweden
27th May	Falkonerteatret, Copenhagen, Denmark
29th May	Congress Centrum Halle, Hamburg, Germany
30th May	Saarlandhalle, Saarbrucken, Germany
31st May	Palais Des Congress, Paris, France
2nd June	Ahoy Hall, Rotterdam, Holland
3rd June	Voorst National, Brussels, Belgium
5th June	St Jacob Stadium, Basal, Switzerland
6th June	?, Innsbruck, Austria
7th June	Sporthalle, Linz, Austria
8th June	Stadthalle, Vienna, Austria
4th September	Perth Entertainment Centre, Perth, Australia
5th September	Perth Entertainment Centre, Perth, Australia

6th September   Apollo Stadium, Adelaide, Australia
8th September   Festival Hall, Melbourne, Australia
9th September   Festival Hall, Melbourne, Australia
10th September Festival Hall, Melbourne, Australia
11th September Festival Hall, Melbourne, Australia
12th September Festival Hall, Melbourne, Australia
14th September Hordern Pavilion, Sydney, Australia

15th September Hordern Pavilion, Sydney, Australia
17th September Festival Hall, Brisbane, Australia
19th September Hordern Pavilion, Sydney, Australia
20th September Hordern Pavilion, Sydney, Australia

4th November   Jai Alai Fronton, Miami, USA
5th November   Jai Alai Fronton, Miami, USA
6th November   Bayfront Centre, St Petersburg, USA
7th November   Atlanta Omni, Atlanta USA
8th November   Municipal Auditorium, New Orleans, USA
9th November   Sam Houston Coliseum, Houston, USA
10th November Dallas Convention Centre Arena, Dallas, USA
11th November Dallas Convention Centre Arena, Dallas, USA
12th November City Fairgrounds, Oklahoma, USA
13th November Municipal Auditorium, Kansas, USA
14th November Milwaukee Arena, Milwaukee, USA
15th November Civic Centre, St Paul, USA

16th November Dane County Coliseum, Madison, USA
18th November Springfield Civic Centre, Springfield, USA
19th November Springfield Civic Centre, Springfield, USA
20th November Nassau Coliseum, Uniondale, USA
21st November Capital Centre, Washington, DC, USA
22nd November Hampton Coliseum, Norfolk, USA
23rd November Greensboro Coliseum, Greensboro, USA
24th November Rupp Arena, Lexington, USA
25th November Hara Arena, Dayton, USA
27th November Civic Centre, Portland, USA
28th November Civic Centre, Hartford, USA
29th November Madison Square Garden, New York, USA
30th November Madison Square Garden, New York, USA

1st December   War Memorial Auditorium, Rochester, USA
2nd December   ?, Wilmington, USA
3rd December   Broome County Veterans Memorial Arena,
                Binghamton, USA
4th December   Providence Civic Centre, Providence, USA
5th December   Philadelphia Spectrum, Philadelphia, USA
6th December   Boston Tea Gardens, Boston, USA

1978

1st May	Usher Hall, Edinburgh, UK
2nd May	Apollo Centre, Glasgow, UK
3rd May	Apollo Theatre, Manchester, UK
4th May	Apollo Theatre, Manchester, UK
5th May	Odeon Theatre, Birmingham, UK
7th May	Rainbow Theatre, London, UK
8th May	Rainbow Theatre, London, UK
9th May	Hammersmith Odeon, London, UK
10th May	Hammersmith Odeon, London, UK
11th May	Hammersmith Odeon, London, UK
13th May	Congresgebouw, The Hague, Holland
14th May	Voorst National, Brussels, Belgium
15th May	Sporthalle, Cologne, Germany
16th May	Stadthalle, Bremerhaven, Germany
17th May	Munsterlandhalle, Munster, Germany
18th May	Deutschlandhalle, Berlin, Germany
20th May	Grugahalle, Essen, Germany
21st May	Friederich Eberthalle, Ludwigshafen, Germany
22nd May	Friederich Eberthalle, Ludwigshafen, Germany
23rd May	Sporthalle, Boblingen, Germany
25th May	Palais Des Congres, Strasbourg, France
26th May	Saarlandhalle, Saarbrucken, Germany
27th May	Olympiahalle, Munich, Germany
28th May	Festhalle, Berne, Switzerland
29th May	Walter Kubel Halle, Russelheim, Germany
30th May	Walter Kubel Halle, Russelheim, Germany
31st May	Kuppelsalle, Hannover, Germany
2nd June	Ostseehalle, Kiel, Germany
4th June	Odeon, Birmingham, UK
5th June	Apollo Theatre, Manchester, UK
1st October	Hampton Roads Coliseum, Hampton USA
2nd October	Capital Centre, Largo, USA

3rd October	Spectrum, Philadelphia, USA
4th October	Spectrum, Philadelphia, USA
6th October	Tea Gardens, Boston, USA
7th October	Tea Gardens, Boston, USA
8th October	Madison Square Garden, New York, USA
9th October	Madison Square Garden, New York, USA
11th October	Madison Square Garden, New York, USA
12th October	Providence Civic Centre, Providence, USA
13th October	Montreal Forum, Montreal, Canada
15th October	Maple Leaf Gardens, Toronto, Canada
16th October	War Memorial Auditorium, Buffalo, USA
17th October	Detroit Cobo Hall, Detroit, USA
18th October	Detroit Cobo Hall, Detroit, USA

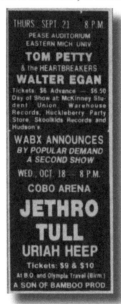

19th October	Checkerdome, St Louis, USA
20th October	Mid South Coliseum, Memphis, USA
21st October	Werner Von Braun Civic Centre, Huntsville, USA
23rd October	Chicago Stadium, Chicago, USA
24th October	Sports Arena, Toledo, USA
25th October	Riverfront Coliseum, Cincinnati, USA

26th October   Pittsburgh Civic Arena, Pittsburgh, USA
27th October   Richfield Coliseum, Cleveland, USA
28th October   Wings Stadium, Kalamazoo, USA

30th October   Veterans Memorial Coliseum, New Haven, USA
31st October   Veterans Memorial Coliseum, New Haven, USA

1st November   Onandaga County War Memorial, Syracuse, USA
2nd November War Memorial Auditorium, Rochester, USA
7th November   McNichols Arena, Denver, USA
8th November   Salt Palace Arena, Salt Lake City, USA
9th November   Centennial Coliseum, Reno, USA
10th November Aladdin Theatre, Las Vegas, USA
12th November Oakland Stadium, Oakland, USA
13th November Inglewood Forum, LA, USA
14th November Inglewood Forum, LA, USA
15th November Long Beach Arena, Long Beach, USA
16th November Long Beach Arena, Long Beach, USA
17th November Long Beach Arena, Long Beach, USA

In-depth Series

The In-depth series was launched in March 2021 with four titles. Each book takes an in-depth look at an album; the history behind it; the story about its creation; the songs, as well as detailed discographies listing release variations around the world. The series will tackle albums that are considered to be classics amongst the fan bases, as well as some albums deemed to be "difficult" or controversial; shining new light on them, following reappraisal by the authors.

Titles to date:

Jethro Tull - Thick As A Brick	978-1-912782-57-4
Tears For Fears - The Hurting	978-1-912782-58-1
Kate Bush - The Kick Inside	978-1-912782-59-8
Deep Purple - Stormbringer	978-1-912782-60-4
Emerson Lake & Palmer - Pictures At An Exhibition	978-1-912782-67-3
Korn - Follow The Leader	978-1-912782-68-0
Elvis Costello - This Year's Model	978-1-912782-69-7
Kate Bush - The Dreaming	978-1-912782-70-3
Jethro Tull - Minstrel In The Gallery	978-1-912782-81-9
Deep Purple - Fireball	978-1-912782-82-6
Deep Purple - Slaves And Masters	978-1-912782-83-3
Rainbow - Straight Between The Eyes	978-1-912782-96-3
Jethro Tull - Heavy Horses	978-1-912782-97-0
Talking Heads - Remain In Light	978-1-915246-01-1
The Stranglers - La Folie	978-1-915246-02-8